LIFE OF

Henry David Thoreau

LIFE OF *Henry David Thoreau*

Henry S. Salt

Edited by George Hendrick, Willene Hendrick, and Fritz Oehlschlaeger

UNIVERSITY OF ILLINOIS PRESS
Urbana and Chicago

First paperback edition, 2000

Manufactured in the United States of America
P 6 5 4 3 2
∞ This book is printed on acid-free paper.

Library of Congress Cataloging-in-Publication Data

Salt, Henry Stephens, 1851–1939.
Life of Henry David Thoreau / Henry S. Salt ; edited by George
Hendrick, Willene Hendrick, and Fritz Oehlschlaeger.
p. cm.
1908 unpublished revision of a work originally published in 1890.
Includes bibliographical references and index.
ISBN 10: 0-252-06906-4 (alk. paper)/ISBN 13: 978-0-252-06906-2
1. Thoreau, Henry David, 1817–1862—Biography. 2. Authors,
American—19th century—Biography. I. Hendrick, George.
II. Hendrick, Willene, 1928– . III. Oehlschlaeger, Fritz.
IV. Title.
PS3053.S3 1993
618'.309—dc20
[B] 95-21567
CIP

He kept the temple as divine,
  Wherein his soul abided;
He heard the Voice within the shrine,
  And followed as it guided:
He found no bane of bitter strife,
  But laws of Love's designing:
He quaffed the brimming cup of Life—
  And went forth unrepining.

—Samuel Arthur Jones

Contents

Acknowledgments

We are indebted to Charlotte Adams for making available to us the papers Salt gave to her husband, Professor Raymond Adams of the University of North Carolina. We have made extensive use of these unpublished papers in the Introduction, including Salt's notes and the letters of Dr. Samuel Arthur Jones, Alfred W. (Fred) Hosmer, Franklin B. Sanborn, and others to Salt. We are also greatly indebted to two friends in England: Jon Wynne-Tyson of West Sussex, Salt's literary executor, for permission to print Salt's previously unpublished letters and notes and to John F. Pontin of Greater Manchester for his continued support of our Salt studies.

Introduction

No Englishman did more in the late nineteenth century to advance the literary reputation of Henry David Thoreau than Henry S. Salt (1851–1939), the remarkable reformer who participated broadly in his era's movements for social change. Salt, who referred to himself humorously as a "compendium of cranks," was firmly committed to what he came to call in his later years "a Creed of Kinship," a "belief that in years yet to come there will be a recognition of the brotherhood between man and man, nation and nation, human and sub-human, which will transform a state of semi-savagery, as we have it, into one of civilization, when there will be no such barbarity as warfare, or the robbery of the poor by the rich, or the ill-usage of the lower animals by mankind." This English Thoreauvian was at once a rationalist, socialist, pacifist, vegetarian, animals' rights activist, prison reformer, naturalist, and conservationist, as well as a biographer and literary critic.[1]

Salt's labors on Thoreau's behalf were many. He published numerous critical articles on Thoreau, commented on Thoreau frequently in his many books, and edited several selections of Thoreau's works: *Anti-Slavery and Reform Papers* (1890), *Selections from Thoreau* (1895), and, with F. B. Sanborn, *Poems of Nature* (1895). Salt's most important work on Thoreau, however, was his biography, *The Life of Henry David Thoreau,* first published by Bentley in 1890 and still regarded as one of the most sympathetic, convincing, and gracefully written biographies of its subject. Salt published a revised version of the *Life* in 1896, incorporating much new information from several American correspondents and omitting many long quotations from Thoreau's letters and *Journal*—sources that had been inaccessible to English readers in 1890. After 1896 Salt continued to receive information about Thoreau from American correspondents, especially Dr. Samuel Arthur Jones and F. B. Sanborn. Salt also gave careful attention to the complete edition of Thoreau's *Journal* published by Houghton Mifflin in 1906. As a result of this new material and research, Salt welcomed the suggestion to revise his biography yet one more time, a suggestion he received from one of his American correspondents, Ernest W. Vickers, in 1906. In January 1908, he wrote Vickers that he had "very carefully revised" his Thoreau biography "in the light of the full *Journals*" and the mass of material he had received since 1896. "The result," Salt added, "is that I have been able to correct and improve the *Life* in many particulars."[2]

Salt met with no success, however, in his attempts to find a publisher for the 1908 biography. As late as 1929, still cherishing the project, he tried again unsuccessfully to interest Houghton Mifflin in the work. At about the same time, Salt began to correspond with a young Thoreau scholar from the University of North Carolina, Professor Raymond Adams, who, apparently at Salt's urging, began gathering materials for his own biography of Thoreau. With characteristic generosity, Salt sent the 1908 revision of his biography and much of his Thoreau correspondence to Adams.[3] Adams's work was never completed, but the 1908 revision of Salt's biography and Salt's Thoreau papers were preserved in Adams's important collection of Thoreau material.

It is the 1908 *Life of Henry David Thoreau,* Salt's final revised biography, that we present here. The work's claims on us are several. First, the revised and improved 1896 edition has long been out of print and thus today is too little known. Secondly, quite apart from its historical interest, the 1908 work, with its finely integrated account of Thoreau's life and ideas, is still a lucid and penetrating introduction to Thoreau's work and thought. Moreover, Salt's own importance to the spread of Thoreau's ideas demands that his last work on Thoreau be known in the final form he gave it. Thoreau was fond of musing on the fruit that would grow from the seeds he had sown. The organic metaphor is important: ideas spread not by being forced on others but through finding a nourishing soil and developing into living, embodied expressions. Salt provided a particularly rich soil for Thoreau's ideas, which he combined with those of others to develop a creed he both believed and lived, the Creed of Kinship, of the covenants between life and life. To read Salt's life or work is to see Thoreau's ideas in the process of assimilation and transformation. His own final reading of Thoreau's life, based on his fullest knowledge of Thoreau's writings, is thus of compelling interest to current and future students of Thoreau.

Later in this introduction we will look at the making of Salt's biography, at how it came to be and how others contributed. But first we need to look at how Salt became the man who read Thoreau the way he did and how his reading of Thoreau played its part in Salt's becoming himself. A child of privilege in Victorian England, Salt was a member of a family tracing its lineage back to King Frederick I of Denmark. After his conversion from respectability to radicalism, Salt viewed his royal ancestry and his own current state wryly:

> A Saxon prince I reigned on earth;
> "The Unready" was my name:
> Less glorious is my second birth;
> Less gay my later fame.
>
> For sceptre, pen; for castle, cot;
> For crown, mere cap on head:
> I'm Author now, not King, and not
> The Unready, but the Unread.[4]

Salt was not born in a castle in Denmark or a mansion in England, but in India, where his father was an officer in the Royal Bengal Artillery. When Salt was a year old, he and his mother returned to England, and Col. Salt was only rarely reunited with his wife and son. Mrs. Salt and Henry lived in the home of her parents in Shrewsbury. Henry's maternal grandfather was a wealthy barrister, and his paternal grandfather, who also lived in Shrewsbury, was a staid banker. Salt was sent to the Reverend C. Kegan Paul, the radical minister, for coaching for Eton. Paul later became a London publisher and was of great help to Salt and other socialists in getting their books into print. Admitted to Eton as a King's Scholar, Salt began the happiest years of his life. He was a successful student at this bastion of the privileged, and for twenty years Eton was the focus of his activities.

Following his early schooling at Eton, his years at King's College, Cambridge, were an unhappy interruption of his Eton life. Later, like Thoreau, who had little good to say about his years at Harvard, Salt spoke of the "ancient pettiness" and the lack of concern for "the higher social ethics" at the university. In addition, the lectures were tedious and the sermons trying. He was a conscientious, even brilliant, student, and he received a first in the Classical Tripos of 1875. At the age of twenty-four he was invited back to Eton as an assistant master, and he settled into a life that promised him economic security and respectability.[5]

Indeed Salt soon discovered that Respectability was the real creed at Eton, that any new and unsettling ideas were banned. His own complacent Respectability was jolted by new, even radical, ideas when during the winter holidays of 1878–79, he met Ruskin through William Harrison Riley, a communist living at Ruskin's St. George's Farm. At a luncheon, Ruskin attacked the hero in Tennyson's "Maud" as "an ass and a fool" and characterized the warlike spirit of the poem as "downright mischievous." The attacks on Tennyson, Salt commented, "sapped the simple faith of an Eton master" (*Seventy Years* 62). Actually, his faith in an age with Darwinism in the air had already begun to erode. He had been bored by the thousands of religious services he had sat through, and his reading of Shelley's poetry and his essay on atheism had given Salt an intellectual basis for his loss of faith in institutionalized religion. Shelley's views on diet reform also influenced Salt's belief in vegetarianism.

Salt's marriage may also have played a part in his revolt from Respectability. In 1879 he married Catherine Leigh Joynes, daughter of the Reverend J. L. Joynes, lower master of Eton. She was a beautiful, emotional, musical person, but she was, Shaw revealed in his preface to *Salt and His Circle,* a lesbian, and the marriage was not consummated. Shaw maintained that the marriage to Kate was the tragedy of Salt's life, but he seems to have overstated the case. Salt was reticent about his personal life and refrained from commenting on his unconventional marriage. From Kate Salt's correspondence, it is obvious that her affairs at times caused great anguish to her husband, but the two shared radical views and indeed had many happy years together.

Through his fellow Eton master and brother-in-law J. L. (Jim) Joynes, Jr., Salt began to meet the social reformers of the day. About 1880 Joynes met George Bernard Shaw in London and brought him to Eton to meet the Salts. An intimate friendship between the Salts and Shaw lasted until Shaw's marriage in 1898, after which Kate was excluded—or excluded herself. Shaw for several years had been Kate's

Sunday husband, and she loved him, he insisted, as much as she could love any man. During the early 1880s Shaw was instrumental in bringing news of the newest reform movements to the Salts.

Jim Joynes also introduced Salt to the Fellowship of the New Life, founded in 1883 by the wandering scholar Thomas Davidson. E. R. Pease, in his classic study *The History of the Fabian Society,* characterized Davidson as "spiritually a descendant of the Utopians of Brook Farm and the Phalanstery, [who] yearned for . . . something in the nature of a community of superior people withdrawn from the world because of its wickedness" (26). Similarly, Ramsay MacDonald, a member of the organization and later to be prime minister, wrote in *Seed-time* for April 1892: "The Fellowship, influenced by Thoreau and Emerson rather than by Marx and Hyndman, stood somewhat aloof, although in sympathy with the ideals of the Socialist societies" (1). The communal aspects of the Fellowship did not appeal to Salt, but the ethical approach, based on Thoreauvian principles, did.

One of the ethical radicals Salt met in his early days as a reformer was Edward Carpenter, who introduced Salt to the works of Thoreau. Carpenter was a Whitmanian as well as a Thoreauvian, and his widely read *Towards Democracy,* directly influenced by Whitman, was admired by many of the advanced thinkers and radicals of the time. The homoerotic overtones of the poem made it a special favorite of those readers in doubt about their sexual identities. Kate Salt called herself an Urning, adopting Carpenter's term. Shaw wrote in the preface to *Salt and His Circle* that Carpenter taught Kate that Urnings were a chosen race. While Carpenter's Whitmanian strain greatly influenced Kate Salt, it was the Thoreauvian strain in his life that had a decisive impact on Henry Salt. Carpenter glorified manual labor and the simple life.[6] Salt wrote Dr. Samuel Arthur Jones on April 12, 1890, that it was through Carpenter "that I first became acquainted with *Walden,* and furthermore was induced to give up my educational work at Eton College . . . and adopt a simpler and more independent style of life."[7]

The Fabian Society grew out of the Fellowship of the New Life. Shaw wrote in *Fabian Tract No. 41:* "The Fabian Society was warlike in its origin: it came into existence through a schism in an earlier society for the peaceful regeneration of the race by the cultivation of perfection of individual character."[8] Though Salt joined the Fabians, his greater sympathies were always with the Fellowship of the New Life and other ethical socialists. Distressed by the factionalism in the socialist movements, he took an eclectic stance, embracing many causes but drawing what he considered the best ideas from each of them. Indeed, he later resigned from the Fabian Society because of its support for the Boer War.

Salt began to meet and move in the circles of such reformers as H. M. Hyndman, William Morris, Sidney Olivier, Graham Wallas, Beatrice and Sidney Webb, Belfort Bax, and Prince Kropotkin. Both Salt and Jim Joynes were in the forefront of the clever young men committed to the socialist and reform movements of the 1880s in England. Their advanced social views were beginning to bring them notoriety at Eton, but Salt's conversion to vegetarianism caused an even greater scandal. Vegetarianism was a particularly suspect "ism" since "it had to be practised as well as preached." Convinced that animals should not be slaughtered and that he no longer wished to be a "cannibal," Salt adopted what he considered to be a saner diet. He found support for his new diet in the works of Shelley and Thoreau.

The beginning of the end of Salt's Respectability occurred when Jim Joynes was forced to leave Eton. Impressed with the ideas of the reformer Henry George, Joynes traveled to Ireland with George in the summer of 1882. George had been arguing in *The Irish Land Question* for the nationalization of land. The Irish police arrested the two as dangerous conspirators and locked them in jail. Once the government discovered its mistake, it apologized to George. Joynes wrote an account of the affair for the *London Times,* causing a scandal at Eton. Later, when Joynes's *The Adventures of a Tourist in Ireland* appeared, the headmaster informed Joynes that he must choose between his mastership and his book. Joynes chose his book, and this action further radicalized him and his brother-in-law.

The conviction was growing on Salt that Eton masters "were but cannibals in cap and gown—almost literally cannibals, as devouring the flesh and blood of . . . animals . . . , and indirectly cannibals, as living by the sweat and toil of the classes who do the hard work of the world."[9] Finally the Salts decided it was time for them to leave Eton, and Salt submitted his resignation to Dr. Warre, the headmaster. Warre attributed Salt's "fall" from Respectability to his conversion to vegetarianism, but upon learning that socialism was also to blame cried out, "Socialism! Then blow us up, blow us up! There's nothing left for it but that!"[10]

The Salts in 1885 moved to a cottage near Tilford where they lived a simple life and began to work for socialist and other causes. Salt contributed political and literary articles and poems to *Justice,* the radical journal published by the Social Democratic Federation. In the November 14, 1885, issue of that journal, Salt published an article on Thoreau in which he argued, "Though not a professed Socialist, but appealing rather to the individual capabilities of man, Thoreau deserves to be attentively studied by every social reformer." Salt believed that many of Thoreau's ideas should appeal to socialists: the simple life and the eschewing of luxuries, the advisability of some education in manual work rather than the "usual flimsy university education," the condemnation of the factory system and the working conditions therein, and the strictures against the "profit-mongering, manslaughtering Railway systems of America" (2). Salt perhaps tried too hard to place Thoreau in the socialist camp, but his article was one of the first sympathetic accounts about the Concordian to appear in England after Robert Louis Stevenson's attack on Thoreau in the *Cornhill Magazine* in 1880.

Thoreauvian ideals appealed to individual socialists and reformers, but the leaders in the Labour movement put little stock in the Concordian who was for individualism, independence, and the simple life. Those leaders who were seeking power looked to theoreticians of reform other than Thoreau.

During the next few years Salt continued to practice the Thoreauvian simple life and to read Thoreau's works and articles about him. He published another essay on Thoreau in *Temple Bar* for November 1886. Combining biography with an analysis of Thoreau's ideas, that essay provided the basis for Salt's first full-length biography. Beginning in 1889 Salt wrote letters to several Americans announcing his intention to write a biography of Thoreau. He assured his correspondents that it was his intention to give a clear account of Thoreau's life and a serious estimate of his doctrines. He wrote to Daniel Ricketson, Thoreau's friend; F. B. Sanborn, who had boarded with the Thoreaus and had published a biography of Thoreau; H. G. O. Blake, Thoreau's literary executor; Dr. Edward W. Emerson, Emerson's son; Col. T. W. Higginson; and many others who had known Thoreau or who were interested in his life and writings. He had useful responses from all of them: reminiscences, references to letters, articles, and books, and offprints.

The two Thoreauvians who gave him the most help were Sanborn and Dr. Samuel Arthur Jones, a Michigan homoeopathic physician who saw a notice of the proposed biography in the *Critic* and contacted Salt. Sanborn copied out for Salt previously published anecdotes of Thoreau, suggested other contacts, and answered specific questions about photographs of Thoreau and about Thoreau's proposal to Ellen Sewall. Jones sent his bibliography of Thoreau and a paper he had published, "Thoreau: A Glimpse."

When writing his 1890 *Life,* Salt had available to him books and articles from the British Museum Reading Room and the materials sent to him by the Americans he had contacted. He made judicious use of biographical facts and drew a full sketch of the life and times of Thoreau. He found much to praise in Thoreau's life, his years at Walden, his struggle to become a writer, his willingness to act on principle. He did not, however, ignore what he considered to be Thoreau's failings: "His lack of geniality, his rusticity, his occasional littleness of tone and temper, his impatience of custom, . . . his trick of overstatement" (247). Salt did not linger, however, on Thoreau's limitations, choosing rather to emphasize his philosophic ideas and his literary abilities.

Salt's evaluation of Thoreau as Transcendental philosopher, naturalist, and writer was the most comprehensive and sensitive of its time. Salt recognized that fundamental to Thoreau's thought was his idealism, distinguishable from Emerson's by a "practicalness" that "had no taste for the subtleties of mere metaphysical abstractions, but made a strong actuality the basis of his reasoning." Salt came to the conclusion, now generally accepted, that Thoreau was not a mere follower of Emerson (217, 218, 219, 220–21).

A central tenet of Thoreau's writing, Salt maintained, was an optimistic belief in human freedom, a belief that largely determined his attitude toward organized religions, government, business, and social institutions. Thoreau's "first demand" was always "that each individual mind, instead of being crushed and warped in the struggle of life, may have space to develop its own distinctive qualities and follow the bent of its own natural temperament." All received values and institutional arrangements "must be examined" and must be discarded when they unnecessarily constrain the free development of the individual. Stressing the importance of Thoreau's essay on civil disobedience with its radical individualist insistence that society be reformed "by individual effort," Salt insisted that Thoreau proposed simplification of life because it lent "strength, courage, and self-reliance to the individual character, and so, in proportion to the extent of its practice, to the State." Salt understood that Thoreau in his simplification was not a mere "nullifier" of civilization. Neither was Thoreau simply opposed to humanitarian reforms, despite his attack in *Walden* on a particular brand of Pharisaical philanthropy; as evidence that he was "one of the humanest of writers," Salt cited Thoreau's denunciation of the Mexican War, his antislavery writings, his "humanity to animals," and his faith in "the humanities of diet" (231, 232, 236, 244–47).

Salt in his subtle analysis of Thoreau's nature writing pointed out that his methods as a naturalist were not those of the "man of science"; instead Thoreau saw the natural world with the inner faculty of the idealist who sought "to transmute the mere facts and results of external observation into symbolical thoughts and images" (248–49). Though Salt emphasized Thoreau's idealist approach to nature, he recognized that the real strength of Thoreau's writing derived from his careful observation of natural phenomena and his insistence on natural fact.

In his consideration of Thoreau's literary craft, Salt praised Thoreau's "unstudied freshness and wildness" of tone, his ability to idealize common and homely subjects in order "to bring to view the latent harmony and beauty of all existent things," and the boldness and novelty of his metaphors. Salt thought Thoreau's pungent epigrammatic style was the "expression of his keen thrifty nature," and he defended Thoreau's use of paradox as a strategy calculated to surprise and challenge the reader. He did grant that the Thoreauvian paradox was sometimes the expression of its author's "wayward and contradictory nature." He found it "inexplicable" that some critics charged that Thoreau had no sense of humour: *Walden,* he said, "is especially pervaded by this subtle sense of humour, grave, dry, pithy, sententious, almost saturnine in its tone, yet perhaps for that very reason the more racy and suggestive to those readers who have the faculty for appreciating it" (256–57, 259, 262, 263–64).

The reviews of Salt's biography of Thoreau were generally favorable, but Jones (somewhat Thoreauvian in his own temperament and one not averse to expressing in the strongest possible way his own views) saw that there were factual errors in the early biographical chapters. Jones had been collecting Thoreauvian printed materials for some time and had wide secondhand knowledge about Thoreau. In the summer of 1890 he traveled to Concord to gather firsthand information. He met Horace Hosmer, a former student of Thoreau's; Eliza Hosmer, daughter of Thoreau's farmer friend; Alfred Hosmer, photographer of Thoreau's haunts and amateur Thoreauvian scholar; Sam Staples, Concord jailer; and many others who had known Thoreau. Jones began to send information to Salt for use in a later corrected edition of the biography. He argued vigorously, to cite one example, that Salt in following Sanborn's comments about Thoreau's mother and father had done an injustice to both of them; Jones's researches convinced him that Mrs. Thoreau was not the village gossip and Mr. Thoreau was not a nonentity.

Jones was entering into an extremely active phase of his Thoreauvian work and sent Salt his articles and books as they appeared: "Thoreau: A Glimpse" (1890), "Thoreau: An Appreciation" (1891), "Thoreau and His Biographers" (1891), "Thoreau's Inheritance" (1893), "Thoreau and His Works" (1894), "Thoreau's Incarceration (As Told by His Jailer)" (1898), *Some Unpublished Letters of Henry D. and Sophia E. Thoreau* (1899)—just to list those of the 1890s—and he also sent along a great deal of other information in his long and lively letters to Salt. Some of Jones's material came by way of Alfred (Fred) Hosmer, who also sent information and photographs directly to Salt.[11]

Sanborn, who visited Salt in England, provided insights, facts, and impressions Salt found useful. In the summer of 1890, Sanborn was in London and Salt had lunch with him on July 12. Salt's notes indicate that Sanborn told him many anecdotes about Thoreau and other Transcendentalists living in Concord—the kinds of stories biographers need to know about their subjects, whether or not they make direct use of them. For instance, the notes indicate that Thoreau "told S[anborn] that wherever he lived he cd. accomodate his taste to the diet of the country. Wd. eat blubber among Esquimaux. He *did* eat some very unappetising Indian messes. He took flesh at his father's table."

Salt's note about that meeting also included this entry on Whitman: "Thoreau & Alcott's visit (the only meeting of T. & W.) They saw him in the bedroom, & both were much impressed with W's personality. Thoreau always spoke admiringly of him. In Emerson's funeral oration there was a sentence in which he enumerated the people whom T. specially admired, omitting himself. These were (1) John Brown, (2) Joe Polis, an Indian guide, & (3) 'one who is not known to those here assembled' [i.e. Whitman]. This sentence was omitted at Sophia Thoreau's request when the oration was printed in the *Atlantic Monthly.* Except for one or two such slight omissions, it was identically the same."

Mr. and Mrs. Sanborn came to afternoon tea and talk from four to six o'clock on July 15, 1890. Salt again made notes. Much of the conversation was about Concord people, and again Salt heard the kind of background information useful to a biographer: Ellery Channing came every Sunday to the Sanborns' "but disappears at any sign of a stranger, even a hat in hall. . . . Will never talk of Thoreau. His immense learning & infallible critical instinct. A wonderful talker, if in the mood, but must be humoured."[12] Sanborn remarked that Edward Hoar was a good talker but less whimsical than Channing. His anecdote about Thoreau's mother was, however, in conflict with Jones's strongly held belief that she was not the village gossip: "Mrs. Hoar was almost as great a talker as Mrs. Thoreau, and when they met, the contest in volubility was great."

Mrs. Sanborn entered into the conversation about the Concordians that afternoon as well. Talking about Thoreau's similarity to Emerson she remarked that she "cd. not tell which was speaking unless she looked at them. There was a trick of speaking of Emerson's—a pausing on the words—which all his friends were liable to adopt. Thoreau's features also resembled E's. Rowse, who made the early portrait of Thoreau, was a young artist who stayed with the Thoreaus. He afterward did better work."

For many years Sanborn wrote Salt long and informative letters about the American Transcendentalists. While Sanborn's failings as a biographer and editor are well known (as Walter Harding and Michael Meyer note in *The New Thoreau Handbook* Sanborn "apparently considered himself a better writer than Thoreau and did not hesitate to take liberties with his manuscript materials"),[13] Sanborn did have a tremendous amount of firsthand information about Emerson, Alcott, and Thoreau, and he was willing to share at least some of this information with Salt.

Salt and Sanborn collaborated on an edition of Thoreau's *Poems of Nature,* published in 1895. Sanborn's letters to Salt indicate that Sanborn took an active role in the work, but Salt wrote Jones that in actuality Sanborn managed to come between himself and Blake, who was in possession of Thoreau's manuscripts, and never sent any new material on to Salt.[14] Salt, a skilled editor, was aware of the many flaws in this edition of Thoreau's poetry.

Salt, a kind and gentle person, managed to stay on good terms with Sanborn, but Jones did not. The fiery doctor, who had served as a physician in the Union Army during the Civil War, was contemptuous of Sanborn, who did not serve. He also believed that Sanborn was not anxious to see Salt's biography of Thoreau appear in the United States because it might reduce sales of his own Thoreau biography. Sanborn does, however, seem to have attempted to arrange with Houghton Mifflin for the publication of Salt's *Life,* but according to him, it was a tardy reader at Houghton Mifflin who was largely responsible for the breakdown of Salt's plan to have his book issued in the United States. Sanborn explained to Salt in a letter of October 10, 1890, that the Houghton Mifflin reader kept the "sheets so long that before I could get them back your book was published in England, and it was no longer possible to issue here simultaneously." Sanborn thought "it needless to offer it to another publisher" but added that he would do so if Salt thought it best. Jones's suspicions seem to have been unfounded.

Salt was in the awkward position of being indebted to Jones and Sanborn. He wrote Professor Raymond Adams on April 14, 1929: "[Dr. Jones] was a good lover, and also a good hater; and his great dislike for F. B. Sanborn made it rather embarrassing for me at times, as F. B. S. was very friendly to me. That is the trouble in all cults, is it not? that the disciples *will* quarrel?"

The late Victorian audience for the biography of Thoreau was a small one. Only eight copies sold in 1891, the year after initial publication. In 1895 when Salt wrote his publisher, Bentley, for permission to revise the biography for inclusion in the Walter Scott series, he noted, "I hope that a cheap edition may be the means of selling some copies of the original one. I am sorry, for your sake as well as my own, that the book fared so badly."[15]

Salt's books consistently had small sales, but that did not keep him from his writing desk. With all the new information and corrections sent him by Sanborn, Jones, and Fred Hosmer, he set to work revising the first edition of the Thoreau biography, making major improvements. In the intervening years, through Salt's own articles on Thoreau in various journals and his editing of several of Thoreau's works, Thoreau had become better known in England and the long quotations from the Letters, Journals, Excursions, etc. were no longer needed. The corrections and stylistic changes Salt made in the 1896 edition of *The Life of Henry David Thoreau* produced a greatly improved volume and one much more readily available in its smaller, inexpensive form.

When the volume reached Ann Arbor, Michigan, Jones wrote one of his typical letters to Salt on April 8, 1896:

> The book has come! It was by my breakfast plate this morning: result, cold coffee but "hot" wife. I am still alive, as this writing showeth.
>
> After seeing my patients (including a twelve mile drive) this morning, I hastened to my private room in my office and sat down to the perusal. I had no dinner, save that I got from the book, which I finished at one sitting literally. (Not the dinner, allow me to explain, but the book.)
>
> Well, you have woven your fabric full of facts; nothing of note that we do know of Thoreau is omitted, and *the* life of Thoreau is now written. In comparing this with the "first edition," I am chiefly impressed by the ever-present sense of Thoreau's presence in the later volume. I lost sight of him too often and for too long periods in your first effort."

The 1896 edition was dedicated to Jones, an honor which, however, did not deter him from penning one lingering complaint: Salt did not put "the maligned Mrs. Thoreau more to the fore." Fred Hosmer, Jones's colleague in Thoreauvian research, concurred in praising the 1896 edition. He wrote Salt on April 22, 1896, that the revised biography "will do a great deal towards correcting the many erroneous ideas in regard to Thoreau." Hosmer noted three factual errors, and he had one additional reservation: "I was glad to find you had corrected your former ideas of Thoreau's parents, but wish it could have been made stronger, for that version of them that Sanborn gave in his Life of Thoreau will be as hard to fight against, and to correct, as Emerson's trying to make Thoreau a 'perfect piece of stoicism.' Miss Ricketson (the daughter of Daniel Ricketson) only the other day in speaking of Sanborn's writing of Mr. & Mrs. Thoreau as he did, said '[it] was perfectly outrageous the way he spoke of them.'"

The revised, improved biography was praised by the reviewers but did not have a large sale. Undaunted, Salt continued his prolific writing and untiring work for good causes. For many years he edited two important journals: *Humanity,* later renamed the *Humanitarian,* and the *Humane Review.* In the next decade he published several books on social issues and was deeply involved in the Humanitarian League, which he helped found. He published widely in the radical and specialized journals on vegetarianism, animals' rights, antivivisection, flogging in prisons and in the Royal Navy, stag hunting, conservation of natural areas, and many other subjects, while keeping up a steady stream of books and articles on literary subjects as well. Salt continued to publish actively in all these areas until well into the 1930s. Both his extraordinary energy and the range of his concerns are illustrated by some of his titles from this period: *Richard Jefferies: A Study* (1894), *Percy Bysshe Shelley: Poet and Pioneer* (1896), *The Song of the Respectables and Other Verses* (1896), *Cruelties of Civilization: A Programme of Humane Reform* (1897), *Kith and Kin: Poems of Animal Life* (1901), *Shelley as a Pioneer of Humanitarianism* (1902), *DeQuincey* (1904), *Animals' Rights Considered in Relation to Social Progress* (1905), *Richard Jefferies: His Life and His Ideals* (1905), *Logic of Vegetarianism* (1906), *On Cambrian and Cumbrian Hills* (1908), *The Ethics of Corporal Punishment* (1909), *The Eton Hare Hunt* (1909), *The Secret of the Reptile House: Snake Feeding at the Zoological Gardens* (1909), *Treasures of Lucretius* (1912), *The Humanities of Diet: Some Reasonings and Rhymings* (1914), *The Flogging Craze: A Statement of the Case against Corporal Punishment* (1916), *David Henry Thoreau: A Centenary Essay* (1917), *Killing for Sport* (1917), *Seventy Years among Savages* (1921), *Animals' Rights Considered in Relation to Social Progress,* revised edition (1922), *The Call of the Wildflower* (1922), *The Story of My Cousins: Brief Animal Biographies* (1923), *Homo Sapiens and Other Verses* (1926), *The Story of Dido and Aeneas* (1926), *The Heart of Socialism* (1927), *The Story of Aeneas: Virgil's 'Aeneid' Translated into English Verse* (1928), *Our Vanishing Wildflowers and Other Essays* (1928), *Memories of Bygone Eton* (1928), *Company I Have Kept* (1930), *Cum Grano: Verses and Epigrams* (1931), and *The Creed of Kinship* (1935).

Sanborn, Jones, and Fred Hosmer went on with their Thoreau investigations and publications, and they kept Salt informed about their work and continued to send him Thoreauvian materials. Fred Hosmer died suddenly in 1903, and that death and the death of Jones's son had disastrous effects on the literary work of Jones. He was able to continue his medical practice, but he gave up his literary correspondence and his writing. Sanborn, however, continued to correspond with Salt, helping especially on Thoreau matters in several 1907 letters.

Thus when Salt began to revise his book for the projected 1908 edition, he had a considerable amount of new material available to him, both in the form of unpublished correspondence from fellow Thoreauvians and printed material. The decade following his 1896 work had been particularly rich in the publication of important works pertaining to Thoreau: Anna and Walton Ricketson's *Daniel Ricketson and His*

Friends (1902); Sanborn's enlarged edition of Ellery Channing's *Thoreau: The Poet Naturalist* (1902); the centenary edition of Emerson's *Works* (1904), with notes by Emerson's son Edward; and Thoreau's *Journal,* published in fourteen volumes by Houghton Mifflin in 1906. Salt made use of all of these sources in drawing his revised portrait of Thoreau in 1908. He made significant cuts throughout the narrative and subordinated contextual material to footnotes, thus keeping Thoreau's presence before the reader even more fully and continuously than in the earlier books. Salt cut from the 1896 volume sections devoted to placing Thoreau within the Transcendentalist movement, thereby achieving greater stress on Thoreau's distinctive individuality. He also reduced the sometimes defensive responses to earlier criticisms of Thoreau. Clearly by 1908 Salt regarded Thoreau as no longer in need of defense. Moreover, Salt included additional factual details on several matters and incorporated quotations from a variety of sources, often giving a quite different emphasis to his interpretation of Thoreau.

In the 1896 *Life,* for example, Salt emphasizes Thoreau's ill-suitedness for teaching; of the private school Thoreau kept with his brother John, Salt writes: "How long Thoreau held this post is not precisely recorded, but it is evident that he did not find his tutorial position at all congenial to his tastes" (30). The passage is deleted from the 1908 edition, replaced by Dr. Edward Emerson's comments: "With regard to the private school of John and Henry Thoreau . . . I collected the testimony, some twenty years [ago], of such of the scholars as I could find, and all but one had remembered it as a privilege of their lives; they loved John and respected Henry." Clearly such evidence suggests that Thoreau had considerably more affinity for teaching than Salt had earlier allowed.

The 1908 *Life* similarly suggests a much different understanding of Thoreau's participation in the family pencil-making business. The 1896 *Life* stresses John Thoreau, Sr.'s, role in devising the process by which the Thoreaus made their levigated plumbago. Henry appears, in contrast, as one who diligently but unenthusiastically applied himself to the business. The 1908 *Life,* however, suggests that Thoreau, in this case as in others, brought some of his own creativity to the solving of life's practical problems. Again citing the "opinion" of Dr. Edward Emerson, Salt indicates that "Henry Thoreau's ingenuity" may have "had a large share in the invention" by which the family made the plumbago. Salt stresses, too, the concern for his family in Thoreau's participation in the business. Here Thoreau works less in compliance with his family's expectations, as the 1896 text implies, and more from the motive of "helping his relatives."

One last example will serve to indicate the way Salt's changes in the 1908 revision contribute to a subtle shifting of his interpretation of Thoreau's character. In discussing Thoreau's lecturing, Salt in 1896 suggested that it was at best "probably a more agreeable" occupation than surveying but that his audience had little interest in his lectures and his delivery was poor: " 'He was a poor lecturer,' says Joseph Hosmer. 'He had no magnetism, and only gave simple dry details, as though he was before a jury to give his evidence under oath. Hence he never succeeded as a platform or lyceum speaker, which I think he desired to be' " (112). In 1908 Salt described Thoreau's lecturing as a "more congenial occupation" than surveying, struck the Joseph Hosmer quotation altogether, and cited a passage from Thoreau's *Journal* in which he describes himself as earnestly offering himself as a lecturer, although without much success. Salt was not content, moreover, to take even Thoreau's account of his lack of success at face value here. Instead he argues that Concord did possess some "who could enter into the spirit" of Thoreau's lectures, as "we know from Dr. Emerson's appreciative reference to 'Thoreau's gift to his townspeople in the old Lyceum, on those dreary winter nights when he read us his 'Wild Apples' or 'Autumnal Tints.' " Salt closes his account, then, not with evidence of Thoreau's lack of popularity as a lecturer but instead with an emphasis on his active participation, over many years, in the Concord Lyceum, where "he gave, in all, nearly twenty addresses" and served "for some years" as "chief organiser of the lectures."

The examples above are just a few of Salt's many revisions of judgment and interpretation in the 1908 work. In addition, he made splendid use of telling new details to reveal aspects of Thoreau's character, as in Thoreau's delightfully cryptic tongue-in-cheek response to one who asks him about a famous crux in *Walden:*

> "Mr. Thoreau, you say in one of your books that you once lost a horse and a hound and a dove. Now I should like to know what you mean by that."
>
> "Why, everybody has met with losses, has he not?"
>
> "A pretty answer to give a fellow!"

Thoreau's humor seems central, too, in Salt's added description of Thoreau's improvised dancing during an 1857 visit to Daniel Ricketson in

New Bedford. In 1896 Salt had emphasized Ricketson's retreat to his own shanty at Brooklawn during the incident, a retreat perhaps motivated by Thoreau's sudden failure to live up to Ricketson's idealized conception of his friend. Now, however, Salt focuses on Thoreau's dancing itself, marked by his "'keeping time to the music carefully but executing some steps more like Indian dances than the usual ballroom figures.'" This vision Salt blends beautifully with Thoreau's later telling his sister Sophia "that in the excitement of this dance he had made a point of treading on the toes" of his companion, "the guileless Alcott, who was sitting on the sofa."

Such are the literary excellences of the 1908 biography, excellences never more apparent than in a note that Salt appends to his penultimate paragraph. As he closes his account of Thoreau's life and writing, Salt simultaneously announces Thoreau's living future. The text points to Thoreau's "steadily increas[ing]" fame on both sides of the Atlantic, an increase caused in part, of course, by Salt's many labors on Thoreau's behalf. Salt's footnote suggests even more important ways Thoreau's life and words will continue to modify the lives of the living, ways not perhaps obvious to historians of literature and literary reputations but well known to one so modified by Thoreau as Henry Salt himself was. As evidence of Thoreau's vitality, Salt writes:

> Witness the splendid "Walden" edition of his works, in twenty volumes, issued by his Boston publishers in 1906. Most noteworthy of all, perhaps, is the testimony of the many simple pilgrims who have been drawn to Concord by love of Thoreau's writings—the student named Harrington, for example, who came from Indiana in 1866, and told Channing that Thoreau's death had grieved him more, though a stranger, than that of any one he had known; or the Russian Jew who emigrated to America through having read some stray leaves of *Walden,* and whose greatest desire in life was to translate the book into his own tongue. It is the vital influence of this sort, far more than current "popularity," that makes its mark in the end.

Despite his diligent work on the 1908 biography, with its excellent focus on Thoreau's timeliness, Salt was unable to find an interested publisher.

Acting as Salt's representative, his American friend Ernest W. Vickers corresponded with at least three firms in the United States—the Public Publishing Company of Chicago, Houghton Mifflin, and

Thomas Y. Crowell—none of which showed any significant interest. From a purely commercial standpoint, the firms who refused Salt's work were undoubtedly correct, for as Salt explained to Vickers, "as many as 2,000" copies of his 1896 book remained unsold in 1908.[16] Salt believed very deeply, however, in the value of his 1908 revision; indeed he was willing to pay a substantial part of the costs for a new edition. He still cherished the idea of publishing the 1908 work as late as 1929, as he remarked in letters to William Sloane Kennedy and to his new correspondent Dr. Raymond Adams of the University of North Carolina at Chapel Hill.

Professor Adams, who had begun his Thoreauvian studies in the 1920s, apparently initiated the correspondence with Salt by sending Salt a copy of his essay "Thoreau and Immortality."[17] Salt wrote Adams on February 13, 1929, that for many years he had put his biography of Thoreau aside but had recently "begun to wonder whether a new and revised edition of it might possibly be launched." (Salt had grieved for almost a decade after the death of Kate Salt in 1919, but in 1927 he married Catherine Mandeville and resumed his writing with renewed vigor. It was soon after his second marriage that Salt turned again to his Thoreau studies.) Once again his efforts failed, as Houghton Mifflin, the American publisher he contacted, indicated that there was a "lack of interest (for selling purposes) in the older biographies." Salt inferred from Houghton Mifflin's response that "a *new* life of Thoreau might be welcomed," and then asked Adams, "If so, who should write one but yourself? If you had the time and inclination, I would gladly send you the various letters, &c. that I possess." Adams wrote Salt on June 20, 1929, that he would undertake to write a biography, and Salt then went through his papers and began to send pertinent items: the 1908 revision of his Thoreau biography; letters by Jones, Fred Hosmer, Sanborn, Blake, and many others; notes; and many miscellaneous items.

We owe to Adams's initiative the clarification of one especially important matter: the nature of the link between Thoreau, Salt, and Gandhi. Adams knew that Salt had met Gandhi, and in response to an inquiry about Gandhi's reading of Thoreau, Salt wrote Adams on September 10, 1929: "I am going to write to Gandhi to ask him if he was influenced by Thoreau." Salt wrote to Gandhi on September 18, 1929, posing that question and ending his letter with the statement that he had been a vegetarian for almost fifty years. Gandhi responded on October 12, 1929: "I was agreeably surprised to receive your letter. Yes, indeed your book which was the first English book I came across on vegetarianism was of immense help to me in steadying my faith in vegetarianism. My first introduction to Thoreau's writings was, I think, in 1907, or late[r], when I was in the thick of [the] passive resistance struggle. A friend sent me Thoreau's essay on civil disobedience. It left a deep impression upon me. I translated a portion of that essay for the readers of Indian Opinion in South Africa which I was then editing, and I made copious extracts from that essay for that paper. That essay seemed to be so convincing and truthful that I felt the need of knowing more of Thoreau, and I came across your Life of him, his 'Walden' and other short essays, all of which I read with great pleasure and equal profit."[18]

When Salt sent a copy of Gandhi's letter to Adams on November 8, 1929, he noted that Mahatma Gandhi had "put the Civil Disobedience principles into *practice* with some effect! Thoreau would have been flattered, had he foreseen." Salt admired the efforts of Gandhi to win Indian freedom and wrote Adams on October 10, 1930: "I should have liked to hear what Thoreau would have said of the present situation in India—a lot of noodles in high places and power, and Gandhi, the *real* power, in prison! Topsy-turvydom indeed!"

Gandhi was in London in 1931, and Salt wrote Adams on November 22: "Last Friday I went up to a crowded meeting in London, when Mr Gandhi was welcomed by a vegetarian audience. As having been connected with his 'conversion' to the vegn. faith, I was seated next to him, and got some talk with him at the end of the meeting. But his time was short, and many persons wished to speak with him; so I was not able to ask him (as I had wished to do) about Thoreau and the essay on 'Civil Disobedience,' by which, as you know, Gandhi was much influenced." Salt understood, as most of his countrymen did not, that civil disobedience was an effective tactic. He wrote Adams on January 3, 1932: "To me it seems most strange that our English rulers should *still* persist in the fatal policy which lost us America, lost us Ireland, and must eventually lose us India also. I managed (for my own satisfaction) to tell Mr Gandhi that I sympathise no less with his Indian policy than with his views on diet."

Gandhi himself began his remarks on November 20, 1931, to the London Vegetarian Society—the meeting to which Salt is referring in his letter to Adams—by clarifying the role of Salt in his belief in vegetarianism. Those remarks comprise a striking tribute to Salt:

"When I received the invitation to be present at this meeting, I need not tell you how pleased I was, because it revived old memories and recollections of pleasant friendships formed with vegetarians. I feel especially honoured [to have] on my right Mr. Henry Salt. It was Mr. Salt's book *A Plea for Vegetarianism,* which showed me why, apart from a hereditary habit, and apart from my adherence to a vow administered to me by my mother, it was right to be a vegetarian. He showed me why it was a moral duty incumbent on vegetarians not to live upon fellow animals."[19] Salt wrote Gandhi on October 8, 1932, referring to Gandhi's speech before the Vegetarian Society: "I feel as strongly as ever that food-reform, like Socialism, has an essential part to play in the liberation of man-kind."[20] To Salt, Thoreau was one of the liberators of mankind, and while he would have profited from hearing Gandhi's comments on the Concordian, he was obviously pleased to hear Gandhi's strong endorsement of vegetarianism.

Salt made one of his last substantial comments on Thoreau and his biography of the Concordian in a letter to Adams on January 1, 1935:

> I have lately been re-reading my own biography of Thoreau, of which, it seemed to me, no further edition will ever be required, as your fuller work will be forthcoming. Much, too, has happened in the forty or fifty years since I wrote; and I should now say that the chief fault of my book was the extreme deference paid in it to the authority of Emerson, as "the seer of Concord," &c. The great value of his friendship to the youthful Thoreau is of course not questioned; but I feel that the time has come when the hard fact has got to be faced, without respect to persons, that the author of "Walden" was (in the long run) the greater man of the two.
>
> It seems unfortunate that Emerson, surviving Thoreau, as he did, should, with the kindest intentions (as his Memoir and editing of the Letters) have contributed to the common belief that Thoreau was one of the lesser lights.

Salt was then eighty-three, and he did not remember that his 1896 biography of Thoreau, strengthened somewhat in the 1908 revision, concluded that "Thoreau's genius will eventually be even more highly valued than Emerson's."

Whether Salt was right in his prediction—one shared by his correspondent Jones—is less important finally than the difference Salt saw between Emerson and Thoreau, a difference that does account for Thoreau's greater appeal to many minds. In a letter of May 11, 1935, to Adams, Salt wrote, again with reference to Emerson and Thoreau: "It is possible for a man to be accomplished, a master of all the arts and sciences, and yet to lack that strange elusive quality which is at last recognised as 'greatness,' and which alone causes a name to live." Salt's language about Emerson is especially revealing here. For Salt, Emerson is a man of accomplishment, a man of letters whose mastery of a great variety of subjects is at once both his strength and his essential weakness. Mastery is only possible over a task that is clearly limited and held at some distance from the self—it depends on a partial withholding of the self. It was this partial withholding of himself from even his most essential commitments that Salt and Jones sensed and objected to in Emerson. For Thoreau, on the other hand, there could be no mastery, as life cannot be mastered. He simply gave himself to living and writing the truth of his life.

Professor Adams was still working on his biography of Thoreau in 1939 when Henry Seidel Canby published his life of Thoreau. Although Canby's book is filled with errors and Professor Adams was a meticulous scholar intent on getting the facts right, Adams believed that there was no room for another life of Thoreau and put his own manuscript aside. It was never to appear. Professor Adams did build a remarkable collection on Thoreau, and we have been able to make use in this edition of the important source material he gathered.

Salt died in 1939, and he had prepared his own funeral address, which contained these words: "I shall die, as I have lived, rationalist, socialist, pacifist, and humanitarian." Had he listed his literary indebtednesses, he would undoubtedly have included Thoreau as one of the greatest of these.

Salt's obituaries recognized many of his unique qualities. The *Daily Telegraph* called him "one of the great characters of his time" and noted that "he was a classical scholar, a wit, and the author of many books, and he took delight in having been regarded as the most thoroughgoing faddist in Britain." Half a century after his death, many people see that Salt's concerns for food reform, for humane treatment of animals, for a more just economic system, for conservation of natural resources are hardly those of a faddist. His perceptive study of Thoreau is also a major achievement deserving a wide audience.

Shaw wrote in his preface to *Salt and His Circle:* "My pastime has been writing sermons in plays, sermons preaching what Salt practised."

In a similar way, Henry Salt wrote essays reflecting major ideas he found in Thoreau: simplification of life, disdain for the accepted religious views and government policies of his time, love of nature, belief in the ethics of civil disobedience. Salt was a Thoreauvian as few others have been, and his 1908 biography is a masterful achievement by one with a deep understanding of Thoreau.

NOTES

1. Salt's remark on the Creed of Kinship here is from the address he wrote for his funeral service; it is quoted in George Hendrick, *Henry Salt: Humanitarian Reformer and Man of Letters* (Urbana: University of Illinois Press, 1977), 1–2.

2. Vickers's letter to Salt of March 1906 is in the Thoreau Collection of the late Professor Raymond Adams, Chapel Hill, North Carolina. It is used with permission of Charlotte Adams. Salt's letter to Vickers is in the University of Illinois at Urbana-Champaign Library.

3. Salt and Adams began to correspond early in 1929. Salt's first letter to Adams is dated February 13, 1929, and his urging Adams to take up the Thoreau work is one of May 3, 1929. Within months afterward, Salt began to send his Thoreau materials on to Adams.

4. Henry S. Salt, *Cum Grano: Verses and Epigrams* (Berkeley Heights, N.J.: Oriole Press, 1931), 142.

5. For biographical information on Henry Salt, see Salt's *Seventy Years among Savages* (London: George Allen and Unwin, 1921); *Company I Have Kept* (London: George Allen and Unwin, 1930); and *Memories of Bygone Eton* (London: Hutchinson, 1928); Stephen Winsten, *Salt and His Circle* (London: Hutchinson, 1951); Hendrick, *Henry Salt;* George Hendrick and Willene Hendrick, eds., *The Savour of Salt: A Henry Salt Anthology* (Fontwell, England: Centaur Press, 1989).

6. For more details, see Hendrick, *Henry Salt.*

7. The letter is printed in Fritz Oehlschlaeger and George Hendrick, eds., *Toward the Making of Thoreau's Modern Reputation* (Urbana: University of Illinois Press, 1979), 70. Salt's letters to Jones are in the Rare Book and Special Collections Library of the University of Illinois at Urbana-Champaign. For additional information about Jones and Salt, see George Hendrick, ed., *Thoreau amongst Friends and Philistines* (Athens: Ohio University Press, 1982).

8. Bernard Shaw, *Fabian Tract No. 41* (London: Fabian Society, 1892), 3–4.

9. Salt, *Seventy Years among Savages,* 64.

10. Ibid., 65.

11. For the contributions of Jones and Hosmer, see Oehlschlaeger and Hendrick, eds., *Toward the Making of Thoreau's Modern Reputation.*

12. Comments in two earlier letters of Sanborn's suggest the difficulties of dealing with Channing. On October 5, 1889, Sanborn urged Salt to write Channing for information about Thoreau but cautioned that Channing "might take no notice of the letter—and all the more if you should mention any one as having suggested your writing; but if you will express pleasure in his Life (a new Edition of which is now printing in Boston) and ask for some explanation of a point or two in it, you may get a very good reply." On October 30, 1889, Sanborn added: "I hope you may get some reply from Mr Channing, but you must not be disappointed if you do not. He mourns for Thoreau constantly."

13. *The New Thoreau Handbook* (New York: New York University Press, 1980), 17.

14. Salt to Dr. S. A. Jones, September 21, 1895, reprinted in Oehlschlaeger and Hendrick, eds., *Toward the Making of Thoreau's Modern Reputation,* 240.

15. John Flanagan, "Henry Salt and His Life of Thoreau," *New England Quarterly* 27 (June 1955): 246.

16. For Salt's correspondence with Vickers, see Fritz Oehlschlaeger, "Henry Salt's Third Biography of Thoreau," *Thoreau Society Bulletin* 146 (1979): 3–4.

17. Adams's essay was published in *Studies in Philology* 26 (1929): 58–66.

18. The Gandhi letter is reproduced in Hendrick, *Henry Salt,* 112.

19. Reprinted in Hendrick, *Henry Salt,* 167.

20. Ibid.

Life of Henry David Thoreau

1

Youth

Of the various perils which beset the path of our modern civilisation, none perhaps are more subtle and dangerous than those which may be summed up under the term *artificiality.* As life becomes more complex, and men of culture are withdrawn farther and farther from touch with wild nature, there is a corresponding sacrifice of hardihood and independence—there is less individuality, less mastery over circumstance, less probity of conduct and candour of speaking, less faith in one's self and in the leading of one's destiny. These may be but incidental disadvantages, outweighed by the general improvement in the condition of the race; yet they are serious enough to demand thoughtful recognition, and to make us welcome any signs of a contrary tendency.

The enormous increase which the present age has witnessed in material wealth and mechanical invention has accentuated both the magnitude of the evil and the necessity of relieving it. A century ago, it might have occurred to those who were living on the threshold of the new era, and who foresaw (as some must have foreseen) the coming rush of civilisation, with its fretful hurry and bustle of innumerable distractions, to wonder whether the very prevalence of the malady would work out its own reformation. Must society ever be divorced from simplicity? Must intellect and wildness be incompatible? Must we lose in the deterioration of the physical senses what we gain in mental culture? Must perfect communion with Nature be impossible? Or would there arise a man capable of showing us in his own character—whatever its shortcomings and limitations—that it is still possible and profitable to live, as the Stoics strove to live, "in accordance with Nature," with absolute serenity and self-possession; to follow out one's own ideal, in spite of every obstacle, with unfaltering devotion; and so to simplify one's life, and clarify one's senses as to master many of the inner secrets of that book of Nature which to most men remains unintelligible and unread. Such anticipation—if we may imagine it to have been entertained—was amply fulfilled in the life and character of Henry David Thoreau.

In the year 1823 there was living in the village of Concord, Massachusetts, with his wife and four children, one John Thoreau, a pencil-maker by employment, whose father, John Thoreau, a younger son in a well-to-do Jersey family of French extraction, had emigrated from St. Heliers to New England in 1773, married a Scotch wife, established a mercantile business in Boston, and died at Concord in 1801.[1] John Thoreau, who at the time of which I speak was thirty-six years old, had begun life as a merchant, but having failed in business and lost whatever property he inherited from his father, he had recently turned his attention to pencil-making, a trade which had been introduced into Concord some ten or twelve years earlier, from which he not only derived a competent livelihood, but gained distinction by the excellence of his workmanship. He is described by those who knew him as a small, quiet, plodding, unobtrusive man, thoroughly genuine and reliable, occupying himself for the most part in his own business, though he could be friendly and sociable when occasion invited. His wife, whose maiden name was Cynthia Dunbar,[2] was very different in character, being remarkable, like the other members of her family, for her keen dramatic humour and intellectual sprightliness; she was tall, handsome, quick-witted; she had a good voice and sang well, and often monopolised the conversation by her unfailing flow of talk.

Henry David Thoreau, the third child of these parents, was born at Concord, 12th July 1817, in a quaint, old-fashioned house on the Virginia Road, surrounded by pleasant orchards and peat-meadows, and close to an extensive tract known as "Bedford levels." In this house, the home of his grandmother, Mrs. Minott,[3] he lived for about eight months; then in a house on the Lexington Road, on the outskirts of the village. In 1818 his parents left Concord for five years, and lived first at Chelmsford, a town ten miles distant, and afterwards at Boston, where Henry first went to school. But as their business did not prosper in either place, the family returned in 1823 to Concord, which thenceforth continued to be their home.[4] They little thought, however, that the name of Concord and the name of Thoreau were destined in later years to be so inseparably associated.

This village of Concord, which lies twenty miles to the north-west of Boston, and must be distinguished from the capital of New Hampshire, which bears the same name, was at the time of Henry Thoreau's boyhood the centre of a scattered township of about two thousand inhabitants. Under the name of Musketaquid it had been an ancient settlement of the Indians, its attraction, in earlier as in later ages, consisting in the rich meadows which border the Musketaquid, or "Grass-ground" river. "When I walk in the fields of Concord," so Thoreau afterwards wrote in his diary, "I forget that this which is now Concord was once Musketaquid. Everywhere in the fields, in the corn and grain land, the earth is strewn with the relics of a race which has vanished as completely as if trodden in with the earth. Wherever I go I tread in the tracks of the Indian." In 1635 the district was purchased from the Indians by the Massachusetts colony, which there made its first inland plantation; and it was from the peaceful settlement then effected that the place received its name of Concord. At the beginning of the last century Concord, though not yet associated with any of the great literary names which have made it famous, was not unknown to the world; for there, in 1775, had been struck the first blow for American independence, when the English troops, after some desultory fighting, were repulsed by the "rebel" farmers. Lafayette visited Concord in 1824, and the following year, half a century after the battle, there was a celebration of that event, at which Henry Thoreau, then a child of seven, is said to have been present.

The inhabitants of Concord were mostly agriculturists—sturdy farmers, living in comfortable old-fashioned homesteads; but there was a considerable sprinkling also of mechanics and men of business; and as the town lay on the high-road between the uplands of New Hampshire and the port of Boston, it was to some extent a centre of trade; it was also at that time one of the places appointed for the holding of the county assizes. A frank and natural equality was one of the traditional characteristics of Concord society, extreme wealth and extreme poverty being alike rare; so that its citizens, a plain and frugal folk, quite unostentatious in their manners and mode of life, yet prizing literature and learning, were saved from the evils of either luxury or destitution; while the well-known Concord families—the Hosmers and Barretts and

Heywoods—preserved and handed on from generation to generation their sterling hereditary qualities. The two leading personages at Concord at the time of Henry Thoreau's birth, and for many years afterwards, were Dr. Ripley, the Unitarian pastor of the village, who lived in the "old Manse" which Hawthorne subsequently inhabited, and Samuel Hoar, a man of senatorial rank,* who exemplified in his character some of the best New England qualities of dignity, justice, and simplicity. Dr. Ripley, quaint, humorous, and patriarchal, was minister at Concord for over half a century, and was regarded by his parishioners as a friend and teacher to whom they could look for advice and assistance in all matters that concerned them. Henry Thoreau was one of the many Concord children who had been baptised by him into the Unitarian Church, and in whose welfare the kindly pastor continued to take an affectionate interest.

The dominant features of the natural scenery of Concord are its waters and its woods; it has been described as "a village surrounded by tracts of woodland and meadows, abounding in convenient yet retired paths for walking." The two rivers of Concord, the slow-flowing Musketaquid and the swifter Assabet, which meet close to the north of the village, have been immortalised by both Hawthorne and Thoreau. "The sluggish artery of the Concord meadows," says the latter, "steals thus unobserved through the town, without a murmur or a pulse-beat, its general course from south-west to north-east, and its length about fifty miles; a huge volume of matter, ceaselessly rolling through the plains and valleys of the substantial earth, with the mocassined tread of an Indian warrior, making haste from the high places of the earth to its ancient reservoir."[5] As for the Assabet, we have it on Hawthorne's authority that "a lovelier stream than this, for a mile above its junction with the Concord, never flowed on earth—nowhere, indeed, except to lave the interior regions of a poet's imagination." Of the Ponds, Walden, Sandy, and White Pond to the south of the village, and Bateman's to the north, are the most considerable; moreover, after the heavy rains, which are usual at two periods of the year, the lowlands adjacent to the river are converted by the floods into a chain of shallow lakes; so that

*Samuel Hoar (1778–1856) was one of Concord's leading citizens. He served several terms in the Massachusetts State Senate and was, from 1835 to 1837, a United States representative. His son, George Frisbie Hoar (1826–1904), served in the United States Senate.—Eds.

there is no portion of the township of Concord which is not more or less in proximity to some lake or stream.

And if well watered, Concord is also well wooded, its sandy soil being covered in almost every direction by thick groves of oak, pine, chestnut, maple, and other forest trees, which even to this day retain much of their primeval severity. "I saw nothing wilder," wrote a visitor to Concord,[6] "among the unbroken solitudes of the Upper Ottawa tributaries than these woods that fringe the bank of Walden. Not a human habitation, not a cleared farm, not a sign of life or civilised occupation anywhere broke the unvaried expanse of wild woodland." The hills which surround Concord—Anursack, Nashawtuck, Ball's Hill, Brister's Hill, and the rest—are of no great height; but they command fine prospects, westward and northward, in the direction of loftier ranges, Wachusett, Monadnock, and the White Mountains of New Hampshire.

"Thoreau's country," says a picturesque writer,[7]

> has the broad effects and simple elements that "compose" well in the best landscape art. It is a quiet bit of country that under the seeing eye can be made to yield a store of happiness. Its resources for the naturalist, at first scarcely suspected, are practically inexhaustible. It is not tame, as an English landscape is tame. It keeps its memories and traditions of the red man along with his flint-flakes and arrow-heads, and its birds and wild-flowers are varied and abundant. A country of noble trees, wide meadow-expanses—and the little river, quiet almost to stagnation, with just current enough to keep it pure, in places much overgrown with water-weed, in other places thick strewn with lily-pads, the banks umbrageous and grassy, fringed with ferns and wild-flowers, and here and there jutting into a point of rocks, or expanding into placid lake-like stretches—these are the main elements of Thoreau's country. Then we must add a clean, sandy soil, through which water percolates with great rapidity, leaving paths pleasant to the feet. Then come the low ranges of hills, the marshes, the ponds, and the forests, fit home for a rich varied wild flora. And then the weather influences must be taken into account. This small district of country, though it feels the breath of the sea twenty miles away, is still somewhat sheltered from the asperities of the east wind. The summer nights are cool and refreshing, though the day may

> have a heart of fire, and the autumn has stretches of bright, cool, resplendent weather. Owing to the dry soil, the ways seem more open and cheery in winter than in other places, and the roads are good for walking all the year round.

Among such scenes and surroundings did Henry Thoreau grow up and receive his earliest impressions of nature and society. From the first he was inured to a hardy outdoor life, driving his mother's cow to pasture when he was a child of six, and going barefoot like the other village boys. School games and athletic sports formed no part of his youthful amusements, but at as early an age as ten or twelve, after the habit of New England boys, he was permitted to shoulder a fowling-piece or fishing-rod and betake himself to the wildest and most solitary recesses of wood or river. The water-side seems to have had a special fascination for him at an early date, one of his childish reminiscences being a visit to Walden Pond, which excited a desire in him to live there, and as he grew older he was fond of bathing and boating on the Concord river in company with his schoolmates, making himself acquainted with all the rocks and soundings of that placid stream. Now and then the news would spread like wildfire that a canal-boat, laden with lime, or bricks, or iron-ore, was gliding mysteriously along the river, and the village children would eagerly flock out to gaze with wonder on these "fabulous river-men," who came and went so unaccountably. Still more interesting were the annual visits of the remnants of some Indian tribes, who used to pitch their tents in the rich meadows which had belonged of old to their forefathers, and there string their beads and weave their baskets, or initiate the Concord youths into the art of paddling an Indian canoe.

We are surprised to learn that, as a child, Henry Thoreau was afraid of thunderstorms, and at such times would creep to his father for protection; for most of the anecdotes related of his school-days are indicative of the fearlessness, self-reliance, and laconic brevity of speech for which he was afterwards conspicuous. At the age of three years he was informed that, like the godly men of whom he read in his religious exercise-book, he too would some day have to die; he received the news with equanimity, asserting, however, that he "did not want to go to heaven, because he could not carry his sled with him, for the boys said it was not shod with iron, and therefore not worth a cent"—a characteristic renouncement of a paradise in which, as he surmised outer appearances would be unduly regarded. When charged with taking a knife belonging to another boy he replied briefly, "I did not take it;" and steadily refused to exculpate himself by further explanation until after the true offender was discovered. All being made clear, the natural inquiry put to him was why he did not sooner explain himself. "I did not take it," was again his reply. When ten years old he carried some pet chickens for sale to a neighbouring innkeeper, who, in order to return the basket promptly, took them out one by one and wrung their necks before the eyes of the boy, who let no word betray the agony of his outraged feelings. His gravity had already earned him among his schoolfellows the title of "the judge"; of that sprightliness of intellect which subsequently showed itself in such a marked degree in his conversation and writings there seems at this time to have been no trace, at any rate no early instance has been recorded.

On the important question of Thoreau's hereditary traits, I quote the following from an interesting article by Dr. S. A. Jones on "Thoreau's Inheritance," which appeared in *The Inlander,* of February, 1893.

> His inheritance included also the endowment of heredity: a potent factor which has not yet had just and due consideration from any of his biographers. A gentleman who attended the school kept by the Thoreau brothers once wrote to me: Henry Thoreau was not a superior scion upon an inferior stock, neither was he begotten by a north-west wind, as many have supposed. There were good and sufficient reasons for the Thoreau children's love of, and marked taste for, botany and natural history. John Thoreau and his wife were to be seen, year after year, enjoying the pleasures of nature, in their various seasons, on the banks of the Assabet, at Fairhaven, Lee's Hill, Walden, and elsewhere; and this too without neglecting the various duties of their humble sphere.
>
> The father was a very cautious and secretive man, a close observer, methodical and deliberate in action, and he produced excellent results. His marbled paper and his pencils were the best in the market, while his stove polish and his plumbago for electrotyping have never, to my knowledge, been excelled. He was a French gentleman rather than a Yankee,[8] and once having his confidence, you had a very shrewd and companionable friend to commune with. Then, when there were no unauthorised listeners about, the otherwise quiet man, who had such a faculty for

"minding his own business," would sit with you by the stove in his little shop and chat most delightfully.

The preponderance of the Saxon, the maternal element in Henry's character, was a matter of observation and comment among his townsfolk. He was a complete New Englander, and prided himself on being "autochthonous" at Concord. "I think the characteristics which chiefly impressed those of us who knew Mrs. Thoreau," says one who was intimate with her, "were the activity of her mind and the wideness of her sympathy. She was an excellent mother and housewife. In the midst of poverty she brought up her children to all the amenities of life, and if she had but a crust of bread for dinner she would see that it was properly served. She was never so poor or so busy that she did not find means of helping those poorer than herself."[9]

We see then that Thoreau was indebted to both his parents for some of his best qualities—to his mother for a quick-witted spirit and passionate love of Nature, to his father for the counterbalance of a calm, sane, industrious temperament, with absolute honesty of purpose and performance. "The marriage of quiet John Thoreau and the vivacious Cynthia Dunbar was a happy conjunction (so it has been well said) of diverse temperaments and opposite traits, of substantial virtues and of simple habits; and with bodies undefiled by luxury, and minds unsophisticated by social dissimulation, they made a home, and its lowly hearth became a shrine whose incense brought blessings to their offspring." It must be added that they entered with such zeal into the agitation for the abolition of slavery, that when that question began to be debated in Massachusetts, they were willing to make their house a rendezvous for abolitionist conspirators.

The younger members of the Thoreau household were also possessed of an unusual strength of will and seriousness of purpose. Both his sister Helen and his brother John, who were Henry's elders by five and three years respectively, were earnest and lovable natures; so too was his younger sister Sophia; and it was remarked by those friends who were intimately associated with the family, that they each possessed a distinctive and unmistakable personality. At this period, when new ideas were permeating American society and preparing men's minds for the great intellectual and social awakening that was shortly to follow, the Thoreaus had won general respect among their neighbours at Concord by their humanity, thoughtfulness, and unaffected simplicity of living.

Here is an early glimpse of Thoreau. It seems that in 1828 they had a Concord Academic Debating Society, and the report of the secretary for November 5th, 1828,* runs thus:—"The discussion of the question selected for debate next followed: *Is a good memory preferable to a good understanding in order to be a distinguished scholar at school?* E. Wright, affirmative; Henry Thoreau, negative. The affirmative disputant, through negligence, had prepared nothing for debate, and the negative not much more. Accordingly, no other member speaking, the president decided in the negative. His decision was confirmed by a majority of four."

In 1833, when sixteen years old, Henry Thoreau was sent to Harvard University,[10] where he occupied a room in Hollis Hall, in which, if we may trust a chance reference in one of his volumes, he experienced the inconvenience of "many and noisy neighbours, and a residence in the fourth storey." He had been prepared for college at the Concord "Academy," an excellent school famous for its successful teaching of Greek, where he had already exhibited a strong liking for the classics, though his reading was not confined to the prescribed course, but began to embrace a considerable extent of English literature. His expenses at Harvard were a serious matter in a family whose means were very limited; the difficulty, however, was surmounted partly by his own carefulness and economy, partly by the help of his aunts and his elder sister, herself a school-teacher at this time. During the college vacations he took pupils, or assisted in school-teaching in several country towns, one of those engagements being at Canton, near Boston, where in 1835, his "sophomore year," he boarded and studied German with a minister named Brownson, at the same time teaching in the "district school."† Meantime his interests at Harvard were being promoted by his future friend, R. W. Emerson, who in 1834 had gone to live at Concord, where his forefathers had held the ministry for generations. Emerson presumably was informed by Dr. Ripley, with whom he was staying, of the promise shown by Thoreau, and it seems to have been due to his

*Walter Harding gives the date of Thoreau's participation in the Concord Academic Debating Society as 1829 rather than 1828; Thoreau's specific engagement with E. Wright took place on November 5, 1829. See *The Days of Henry Thoreau* (New York: Alfred A. Knopf, 1970), 28.—Eds.

†Thoreau taught only in Canton, not in several country towns. See Harding, *The Days of Henry Thoreau,* 45–46.—Eds.

good offices that the young man received some small pecuniary assistance from the beneficiary funds of the college, where he graduated in 1837.

We are fortunate in having a graphic account of Thoreau's personal appearance and mode of life at Harvard from the pen of one of his classmates.[11] It seems that he passed for nothing among his companions, taking little share in their studies and amusements, shunning their oyster suppers and wine parties, and mysteriously disappearing from the scene when, as occasionally happened, the course of college discipline was temporarily interrupted by a "rebellion."

> He was cold and unimpressible. The touch of his hand was moist and indifferent, as if he had taken up something when he saw your hand coming, and caught your grasp upon it. How the prominent grey-blue eyes seemed to rove down the path, just in advance of his feet, as his grave Indian stride carried him down to University Hall. He did not care for people; his class-mates seemed very remote. This reverie hung always about him, and not so loosely as the odd garments which the pious household care furnished. Thought had not yet awakened his countenance; it was serene, but rather dull, rather plodding. The lips were not yet firm; there was almost a look of smug satisfaction lurking round their corners. It is plain now that he was preparing to hold his future views with great setness and personal appreciation of their importance. The nose was prominent, but its curve fell forward without firmness over the upper lip, and we remember him as looking very much like some Egyptian sculptures of faces, large-featured, but brooding, immobile, fixed in a mystic egoism. Yet his eyes were sometimes searching as if he had dropped, or expected to find, something. In fact his eyes seldom left the ground, even in his most earnest conversations with you.
>
> He would smile to hear the word "collegiate career" applied to the reserve and inaptness of his college life. He was not signalised by the plentiful distribution of the parts and honours which fall to the successful student. Of his private tastes there is little of consequence to recall, except that he was devoted to the old English literature, and had a good many volumes of the poetry from Gower and Chaucer down through the era of Elizabeth. In this mine he worked with a quiet enthusiasm.

These traits of aloofness and self-seclusion are attributed by his classmate not to any conceit or superciliousness, still less to shyness, but to a sort of homely "complacency," which, though quite natural and inevitable, had the effect of putting him out of sympathy with his surroundings at Harvard. Thus he is said to have worn a green coat at College, "because the authorities required a black one." His complacency was "perfectly satisfied with its own ungraciousness, because that was essential to its private business." This determined concentration on his own life-course was, as we shall see, very characteristic of Thoreau in his mature career, and it is interesting to find that it was thus early developed.

"In college Thoreau had made no great impression," says another of his contemporaries;[12] "he was far from being distinguished as a scholar, was not known to have any literary tastes, was never a contributor to the college periodical, *Harvardiana;* he was not conspicuous in any of the literary or scientific societies of the undergraduates, and withal was of an unsocial disposition, and kept himself very much aloof from his class-mates. At the time we graduated, I doubt whether any of his acquaintances regarded him as giving promise of future distinction." Against this, however, must be set what the historian of Thoreau's college class wrote in 1887, that "notwithstanding what he himself says of his entrance to the college, and the impression that one gets from some of his biographers that he was rather under the ban of the authorities, Thoreau maintained a very fair rank in his class, and at graduation took part in a Conference on the 'Commercial Spirit of Modern Times.' "[13] This was somewhat of an honour; and there is no reason to suppose that Thoreau had any part in the "rebellions" and other irregularities of the students, as has sometimes been suggested.

We can well believe, however, that his strong individualist tendencies had even now begun to manifest themselves; indeed it is apparent from his youthful "themes" that he was already a fearless thinker and questioner on various matters, social and religious—a quality which would not be likely to conciliate the good opinion of the college authorities. His integrity, however, and high moral principle were clearly recognised; and from the first he seems to have practised a simple and abstemious mode of living. "He had been so wisely nourished at the collegiate fount," says Channing, "as to come forth undissipated, not digging his grave in tobacco and coffee—those two perfect causes of paralysis." Thoreau has himself stated that he never smoked anything more noxious than dried lily-stems, from which indulgence he had a faint recollection of deriving pleasure before he was a man.

It has been said that Thoreau's debt to his College was important; but this is a statement which it will be prudent to accept with some reservation. It is true that although not "successful," in the ordinary sense of the word, he had become a good classical scholar, and had derived intellectual benefit from the teaching of at least one of the lecturers, Professor Channing, whose nephew, Ellery Channing, afterwards became his most intimate friend. He himself says in a letter of 1843 that what he learned in College was chiefly "to express himself," and this, in his case, was certainly no unimportant gift. But, on the whole, we shall probably be safe in concluding that the advantages which Thoreau obtained from his college career were mainly of the indirect kind, and that he profited far less by the actual instruction there given him than by the opportunities afforded for wide reading and self-culture.

Meantime his love of outdoor life and open-air pursuits had in nowise diminished during his residence at Harvard; on the contrary, he was as diligent a student of natural history as of rhetoric or mathematics, and felt as much veneration for Indian relics as for Greek classics; more so, if we are to believe what he wrote subsequently in a letter to the Class Secretary.[14] "Though bodily I have been a member of Harvard University, heart and soul I have been far away among the scenes of my boyhood. Those hours that should have been devoted to study have been spent in scouring the woods and exploring the lakes and streams of my native village. Immured within the dark but classic walls of a Stoughton or a Hollis, my spirit yearned for the sympathy of my old and almost forgotten friend, Nature." It is stated that his first experiment in camping-out took place during his senior year at college, when he made an excursion of this sort to Lincoln Pond, a few miles from Walden. On this occasion his companion was Stearns Wheeler, one of his schoolmates both at Concord and Harvard, whose early death in 1843 is lamented in one of his letters.

But undoubtedly it was in his conception of ethical principles, together with a kind of mystic nature-worship, that he had made the greatest progress towards maturity of thought. We are told that he resolved at an early period of his life, probably during his college career, "to read no book, take no walk, undertake no enterprise, but such as he could endure to give an account of to himself; and live thus deliberately for the most part." When only seventeen he had become convinced of the utility of "keeping a private journal or record of thoughts, feelings, studies, and daily experience," with a view to "settling accounts with one's mind"—an introspective tendency which grew stronger and stronger with increasing years. Already, too, his intense ideality of temperament was clearly developing itself; while still a boy he had written that "the principle which prompts us to pay an involuntary homage to the infinite, the incomprehensible, the sublime, forms the very basis of our religion." It was his delight, as he tells us, to monopolise a little Gothic window overlooking the garden at the back of his father's house, which stood on the main street of Concord village, and there, especially on Sunday afternoons, to muse in undisturbed reverie. Often in the early dawn he would stroll with his brother John, to whom he was devotedly attached, to the "Cliffs," a rocky ridge which overhangs the river Concord, and there watch the sunrise over the expanse of Fairhaven Bay.

His devotion to Concord was already a fixed and unalterable sentiment, which sometimes showed him in a softer and more emotional mood than was usual to his self-repressed nature. While he was still at college he happened one day to ask his mother what profession she would advise him to choose. She replied that he could buckle on his knapsack and roam abroad to seek his fortune in the world. The tears rose to his eyes at this suggestion, and his sister Helen, who was standing by, tenderly put her arm round him, and said, "No, Henry, you shall not go; you shall stay at home and live with us." So fully were these words verified that twenty years later we find him still living at Concord, and writing to one of his friends that he had "a real genius for staying at home."

NOTES

1. It is said that the name Thoreau was common in the annals of Tours several hundred years ago, as it still is on gravestones in Jersey. The emigrant above mentioned, John Thoreau, son of Philip Thoreau and Marie le Galais, kept up some correspondence with his brother, Peter Thoreau, who remained at St. Heliers, but after the death of Peter, about 1810, all communication between the two branches of the family came to an end. An interesting account of the Jersey Thoreaus appeared in the *Boston Evening Transcript* of February 8, 1896.

2. Her father, the Rev. Asa Dunbar of Keene, New Hampshire, died in 1787, and his widow afterwards married a Concord farmer named Minott. In Mrs. Thoreau's brother, Charles Dunbar, the ready wit, characteristic of the Dunbar family, had run to eccentricity. He led a strange vagabond life, roving from town to town, and winning a pot-house notoriety by his waggish speeches and dexterity in wrestling and conjuring.

3. The "Minott house" has been removed to another situation, but its features have been well preserved in a sketch by Miss Wheeler.

4. For a list of the various houses in Concord occupied, or built, by the Thoreaus, see Thoreau's *Journal,* December 27, 1855.

5. Introduction to *The Week.* Compare Hawthorne's account in *Mosses from an Old Manse.*

6. Grant Allen, in *Fortnightly Review,* May 1888.

7. "A. L.," in *New York Evening Post,* October 10th, 1890.

8. The name Thoreau, though now Yankeefied, was pronounced by those who knew the family in Concord as a spondee Thōreau̅. See Lowell's "Fable for Critics," where, after satirising Ellery Channing as a plagiarist poet who would have robbed Emerson's apple-orchard, he adds: "Besides, 'tis no use, you'll not find e'en a core; / Thoreau has picked up all the windfalls before."

9. E. M. F., in *Boston Daily Advertiser,* February 18th, 1883. I must plead guilty to having done less than justice to Thoreau's parents in the first edition of this book.

10. He is entered in the Harvard register as he was christened, David Henry Thoreau; but he afterwards put the more familiar name first.

11. Rev. John Weiss, *Christian Examiner,* Boston, July 1865.

12. The Rev. D. G. Haskins, in his *Ralph Waldo Emerson,* Boston, 1887.

13. See *Familiar Letters,* p. 8.

14. *Memorials of the Class of 1837.* By Henry Williams, Boston, 1887.

2

Early Manhood

When Thoreau left the University he was just twenty years old, and the first question which occupied his mind was naturally the choice of a profession by which he might gain his living. Like the other members of his family he became a teacher, an occupation of which he had, as we have seen, already made trial during his vacations at college. "Kept town school a fortnight in 1837," he records in his Journal, this being a sort of grammar school which had been established by Concord citizens.

If we may trust the humorous account given by Ellery Channing of Thoreau's pedagogic experiences, the immediate cause of the resignation of this office was the question of corporal punishment. He at first announced that he should not flog, but should substitute the punishment of "talking morals" to his pupils; but after a time one of the School Committee remonstrated against this novel system, and protested that the welfare of the school was being endangered by the undue leniency of its master. Mr. Thoreau must use the ferule, or the school would spoil. "So he did, by feruling six of his pupils after school, one of whom was the maid-servant in his own house.[1] But it did not suit well with his conscience, and he reported to the Committee that he should no longer keep their school, as they interfered with his arrangements." In the spring of 1838 he went on a visit to Maine, where his mother had relatives, on the look-out for some educational appointment, bearing with him testimonials signed by Dr. Ripley, R. W. Emerson, and the President of Harvard University. He seems, however, to have been unsuccessful in this particular quest; for in the same year we find him engaged with his brother in keeping a private school for boys and girls.[2] School-keeping seems to have been practised by Thoreau for about two years in all;* then, as more congenial subjects occupied his attention, he gave it up altogether, and betook himself to his foreordained and inevitable profession—the study of nature. The ferule of the schoolmaster was laid by for the herbarium and spy-glass of the poet-naturalist.

This brings us to the mention of a movement which was gathering force in New England during Thoreau's youth and early manhood, and had a marked influence on the whole development of his character. Transcendentalism (i.e., the study of the pure reason which *transcends* the finite senses, the "feeling of the infinite," as Emerson expressed it), which originated in the philosophy of Kant, and was revived by Coleridge and Carlyle in England, had now begun to be a disturbing and regenerating power in American thought, and to find its chief exponents in such men as George Ripley, Alcott, and Emerson; though there had long before been a vein of native transcendentalist doctrine in the quietism and quakerism of Penn, John Woolman, and others. The transcendentalism of New England was simply a fresh outburst of ideal philosophy; it was a renaissance in religion, morals, art, and politics; a period of spiritual questioning and awakening. "The transcendental movement," says Lowell, "was the protestant spirit of Puritanism seeking a new outlet and an escape from forms and creeds which compressed rather than expressed it." The "apostles of the newness," or "realists," as the transcendentalists were variously styled, aimed at a return from conventionality to nature, from artifice to simplicity; they held that every one should not only think for himself, but should labour with his own hands; and the exaltation of the individual, as opposed to the State and the territorial immensity of America, was one of their most cherished purposes.

It was not to be expected that this transcendentalist revival, which by its very nature was vague, misty, and ill-defined, would be exempt from the extravagances and absurdities which almost inevitably accompany such a movement. But if certain members of the transcendentalist party were deservedly the butt for a good deal of ridicule, the main

*Actually the Thoreau school lasted closer to three years. It opened in mid-June 1838 and closed April 1, 1841. See Harding, *The Days of Henry Thoreau,* 75–87. —Eds.

purpose of the movement was too important to be laughed down, and fully justified itself in the light of subsequent events. Originating in the meetings of a few friends, of whom Emerson was one, at George Ripley's house in Boston, this New England transcendentalism proved to be one of the most powerful forces in American literature and politics.

Concord, where Thoreau was born and bred, became, as we shall see, one of the centres of the transcendental movement, which aimed at carrying its doctrines into every branch of social life; it is not surprising, therefore, that a mind already naturally predisposed to idealism should have been strongly affected by the congenial gospel of an inner intellectual awakening. His diaries, poems, and early letters are full of this transcendental tone; and it was doubtless in great part owing to the same influence that he felt so marked a disinclination to settle down in the ordinary groove of business.

It was under the stress of this new faith that in 1838, or thereabouts, while he was still a school teacher, he had quietly but definitely seceded from Dr. Ripley's congregation. The youthful secessionist had moreover run the risk of imprisonment by his refusal to pay the church-tax, on the ground that he did not see why the schoolmaster should support the priest more than the priest the schoolmaster. The difficulty was finally settled by his signing a statement in which he testified that he was not a member of any congregational body. That so fearless and independent a thinker as Thoreau should maintain his adherence to any religious formula was not to be expected, for the very reason that the natural piety of his mind was so simple and sincere. If a name be sought for the faith which he henceforth held and practised, he should probably be styled a pantheist. Never was there a more passionately devout worshipper of the beauty and holiness of Life, and it was on this instinctive belief in the eternal goodness of Nature that he based the optimistic creed which we shall find to be the central point of his philosophy.

The question of a profession, it may well be supposed, was pressed on the youthful enthusiast by anxious relatives and friends. As we have already seen, pencil-making was the regular employment of the Thoreau family, and Henry, like his father, acquired much skill in this handicraft, to which he applied himself at intervals, during the greater portion of his life, by way of helping his relatives. The story goes that when he had entirely mastered the secrets of the trade, had obtained certificates from the recognised connoisseurs in Boston of the excellence of his workmanship, and was being congratulated by his friends on having now secured his way to fortune:—he suddenly declared his intention of making not another pencil, since "he would not do again what he had done once." True or not, the anecdote is happily characteristic of Thoreau's whimsical manner of expressing his most serious convictions.

It was, however, less on pencil-making than on a special preparation of plumbago that the Thoreaus depended, their secret consisting in the process. Dr. E. W. Emerson is of opinion that Henry Thoreau's ingenuity had a large share in the invention. "The new art of electro-typing demanded the best plumbago, and the Thoreaus had practically the monopoly by the excellence of their lead." It is certain that Henry Thoreau made the levigated plumbago long after the pencil-making had ceased.

He had early discovered that what is called "profit" in commercial life is often far from being, in the true sense, profitable; that the just claims of leisure are fully as important as the just claims of business; and that the surest way of becoming rich is to need little: in his own words, "a man is rich in proportion to the number of things which he can afford to let alone." This being so, why should he, at the outset of his career, pledge himself irrevocably, after the manner of young men, to some professional treadmill, and for the sake of imaginary "comforts" sacrifice the substantial happiness of life? "No, no," he exclaims, at a later period, in reply to a well-meant suggestion that, being without a definite profession, he should engage in some commercial enterprise; "I am not without employment at this stage of the voyage. To tell the truth, I saw an advertisement for able-bodied seamen, when I was a boy, sauntering in my native port, and as soon as I came of age, I embarked." This enterprise was none other than the study of wild nature; his "business" was to be a professional walker or "saunterer," as he called it; to spend at least one half of each day in the open air; to watch the dawns and the sunsets; to carry express what was in the wind; to secure the latest news from forest and hill-top, and to be "self-appointed inspector of snow storms and rain storms." These duties he subsequently declared that he had faithfully and regularly performed; if his friends were disappointed, he at least was not. Witness his own lines in his poem, "Prayer"—

Great God, I ask thee for no meaner pelf
Than that I may not disappoint myself,
That in my action I may soar as high
As I can now discern with this clear eye.

And next in value, which thy kindness lends,
That I may greatly disappoint my friends,
Howe'er they think or hope that it may be,
They may not dream how thou'st distinguished me.

Idleness, however, formed no part of Thoreau's "loitering"; he was not one who would permit himself to be dependent on the labour of others; for he was well aware that one of the most significant questions as to a man's life is "how he gets his living, what proportion of his daily bread he earns by day labour or job work with his pen, what he inherits, what steals." Apart from the chosen occupation of his lifetime, to which he devoted himself with unflagging industry and zeal, he conscientiously supported himself by such occasional labour as his position required, toiling from time to time (to quote an illustration which he was fond of using) like Apollo in the service of Admetus. During the first ten years of his mature life, that is from 1837 to 1847, he earned what little he needed chiefly by manual work, his remarkable mechanical skill enabling him to do this with readiness. Land-surveying was another employment in which he incidentally busied himself; and here too, owing to his adroitness in mensuration, and his intimate acquaintance with the Concord hill-sides and "wood-lots," his services were highly valued.

He had also begun, though but slightly and tentatively at first, to give his attention to lecturing and literary work. His first lecture, the subject of which was "Society," was delivered in April 1838, at the Concord "Lyceum," where he afterwards lectured almost every year during the remainder of his life. His earliest poems were composed about 1837. While in residence at Harvard University he had been a constant reader of verse, had mastered Chalmers' Collection, and become acquainted with a quaint and old-fashioned school of poetry little known to his neighbours and contemporaries. The influence of Herbert, who was one of his early favourites, is very discernible in Thoreau's youthful poems, and Cowley, Davenant, and Donne were most attentively studied by him; Quarles also, at a somewhat later period. One of the most remarkable of these early poems is the piece entitled "Sic Vita," of which the first stanza runs thus—

> I am a parcel of vain strivings, tied
> By a chance bond together,
> Dangling this way and that, their links
> Were made so loose and wide,
> Methinks,
> For milder weather.

This poem was written on a strip of paper which bound together a bunch of violets, and so thrown in by Thoreau at the window of Mrs. Emerson's sister, Mrs. Lucy C. Brown, of Plymouth, a lady with whom he corresponded, and who was the means, as will be related, of his being introduced to Emerson. In 1837 a strong stimulus was given to his prose writing by the commencement of a regular series of diaries, the first of which, the *Red Journal,* ran on to some six hundred long pages in less than three years. Here he systematically noted his daily walks, adventures, and meditations, so that as the diary was revised and corrected with considerable minuteness, its author was able to draw direct from this literary store whenever he needed the materials for a poem or essay. This was the case with his contributions to the *Dial,* when that transcendentalist organ was started in 1840 by certain of Thoreau's friends.

At this time there were living in the Thoreaus' house at Concord a Mrs. Ward, widow of Colonel Joseph Ward, an officer who distinguished himself in the War of Independence, and her daughter, Miss Prudence Ward, who is referred to in an early passage of Thoreau's first volume, *The Week,* as the friend to whom the two voyagers sent news of the whereabouts of the rare hibiscus. The Wards and the Thoreaus had been old friends in Boston, when both families were living there; and Mrs. and Miss Ward had come to Concord in 1833, living first with Henry Thoreau's aunts, Jane and Maria Thoreau, and afterwards at the house of his father. This led to an incident which must have affected him very deeply at the time, and may possibly furnish a key to some otherwise obscure traits in his writings—his love for the girl to whom his brother John is also said to have been attached. This was Ellen Sewall, a granddaughter of Mrs. Ward, and daughter of the Rev. E. Sewall, pastor of Scituate. Her two brothers were at school at Concord under John and Henry Thoreau,* and Ellen, a beautiful girl of seventeen, used to visit the Thoreaus in order to be near her relatives. These visits were much enjoyed by all the party, as the four younger members of the Thoreau household were then at home; and many hours were pleasantly spent in long country walks or boating-excursions, or in reading aloud and discussing, according to a custom then popular in Concord, some book in which they were interested.

Hence it happened that the two brothers fell in love with Ellen Sewall; and the story has been told that Henry, in a rare spirit of self-sacrifice, abstained from urging his own claims, so as to avoid placing himself in any rivalry with his brother. There is, however, no reason to believe that the girl felt anything more than friendship for either of them, and shortly after John Thoreau's death she married the man of her choice, a clergyman, with whom she lived happily to a good old age.

Thoreau's elegiac stanzas, first recorded in his Journal, June 24, 1839, under the title of "Sympathy," are said, on Emerson's authority, to contain a reference, under a thin disguise, to his love for Ellen Sewall, the "gentle boy" of the poem being in truth a gentle girl; but, according to another statement, the verses were dedicated to her brother, Edmund Sewall, a boy of great promise and most lovable disposition, who bore a strong likeness to his sister.[3]

Lately, alas! I knew a gentle boy
Whose features all were cast in Virtue's mould,
As one she had designed for Beauty's toy,
But after manned him for her own stronghold.

So was I taken unawares by this,
I quite forgot my homage to confess;
Yet now am forced to know, though hard it is,
I might have loved him, had I loved him less.

Each moment as we nearer drew to each,
A stern respect withheld us further yet,
So that we seemed beyond each other's reach,
And less acquainted than when first we met.

*Edmund Sewall was a student in the Thoreaus' school. Whether his brother, George, was also a student there is in doubt. In a letter to the editors of this volume, Walter Harding says that George was not a student of the Thoreaus.—Eds.

Eternity may not the chance repeat;
But I must tread my single way alone,
In sad remembrance that we once did meet,
And know that bliss irrevocably gone.

To those who are acquainted with even the outline of this story of Thoreau's youthful passion, it becomes less difficult to understand the somewhat severe and remotely ideal tone that pervades his utterances on friendship and love. In this relation we see that there is a peculiar appropriateness in the title which Emerson applied to Thoreau—the "Bachelor of Nature."[4]

That Thoreau would have been willing to make any sacrifice of his personal happiness for the sake of his brother, we can well believe; for this brother was, as he has gratefully recorded, his "good genius," a "cheerful spirit" by whose sunny presence he was ever invigorated and reassured. The two had been intimately associated from childhood, had worked together and played together, and roamed in company over all the hills and woodlands of Concord. It was with his brother John that Henry made, in 1839, that famous holiday-trip on the waters of the Concord and Merrimac[k] rivers, an account of which was published, ten years later, in *The Week.* Starting from Concord on the last day of August, in their boat, the *Musketaquid,* which they had made with their own hands in the spring, and taking with them their tent, guns, fishing-tackle, and various provisions for the voyage, they journeyed down the slow-flowing Concord river, till they came to its confluence with the larger and swifter Merrimac[k] at Lowell. Thence they rowed up the stream of the Merrimac[k], which, by comparison with that which they had left, seemed like "a silver cascade which falls all the way from the White Mountains to the sea," until they arrived within a few miles of the New Hampshire capital, which bears the same name as their native village. Here they were compelled to leave their boat, while they proceeded on foot along the bank of the narrowing stream, and so traced the Merrimac[k] river to its source among the White Mountains.

Up to the date of which we are speaking he had no very intimate companion except his brother John, for he had made no close friendships at college, such as should last him for a lifetime. One friendship, however, had already commenced, which was of extreme value to him both in itself and as being the means of introducing him to a larger circle of friends. Emerson, as has been stated, had settled in Concord in

1834, and had at once manifested a kindly interest in the welfare of his young neighbour, fifteen years his junior,* who was then studying at Harvard University. It was probably in 1837 that their first personal meeting, which could not long have been delayed, was brought about through the agency of Emerson's sister-in-law, who, having been informed by Helen Thoreau that there was a passage in her brother Henry's diary which contained some ideas similar to those expressed by Emerson in a recent lecture, reported the matter to Emerson, and at his request brought Henry Thoreau to his house. Thus began an intercourse which continued almost unbroken during the rest of Thoreau's life, and was productive of much pleasure and profit on both sides, to the elder man as well as to the younger. "I delight much in my young friend," wrote Emerson in 1838, "who seems to have as free and erect a mind as any I have ever met."

The value to Thoreau of this admission into the Emersonian circle, exactly at the time when he was able to derive from it the most advantage and encouragement, can hardly be over-estimated; for not only did it draw out the latent energies of his character, but gave him an opportunity of expressing and publishing his thoughts. A periodical which should be the accredited organ of the new ideas had for some time been in contemplation among the members of the transcendental "symposium," and in 1840 this project was carried into effect by the establishment of the quarterly *Dial,* the management of which was chiefly in the hands of Emerson, Margaret Fuller, and George Ripley. Its chances of success, in the commercial sense, were from the first very precarious, for the number of original subscribers was small, and a transcendental magazine was not likely to attain to much popularity; but the *Dial* was nevertheless the means of uniting the advocates of the new philosophy, and of affording an opening for many writers of merit who had been hitherto unknown. Commencing in July 1840, it continued to be issued for four years, the editorship during the first half of that time being entrusted to Margaret Fuller and George Ripley, while among the contributors were Emerson, Alcott, Margaret Fuller, Ripley, Theodore Parker, Elizabeth Peabody, Lowell, Thoreau, Ellery Channing, Jones Very, W. H. Channing, and many others of more or less note. Each of the four volumes of the *Dial* contained essays and poems from Thoreau's

*Emerson was born May 25, 1803, and Thoreau July 12, 1817; Emerson was thus more nearly fourteen than fifteen years Thoreau's senior.—Eds.

pen, his poem on "Sympathy" in the first number being his earliest appearance in print.* This, however, was but his novitiate in literary work, and several of his papers were rejected by Margaret Fuller, during the term of her editorship, with a candid criticism of what she judged to be their crudities and defects.

The presence of Emerson at Concord, to which place he was bound by family ties and early associations—four of his ancestors having been Concord ministers and Dr. Ripley being his step-grandfather—was an event of no slight importance in the history of that somewhat secluded township. After resigning his Unitarian pastorate at Boston in 1832, and spending the next year in England, he had married his second wife, Miss Lydia Jackson, and taken up his permanent residence at Concord in 1835,† where he was so clearly recognised as its most illustrious citizen that in 1836, when a monument was erected on the site of the battlefield of 1775, he was chosen to commemorate the occasion by the stanzas which have since become so celebrated. Through the rise of transcendentalism and the rapid spread of Emerson's literary fame, Concord—such is the attraction of genius—became more and more a place of note and the resort of poets and philosophers.

Prominent among these was Amos Bronson Alcott, who came to Concord with his wife and daughters in 1840, tall, slender, white-headed, one of the gentlest and most lovable of men, and highly valued by Emerson, as by all who knew him (smile though they might at his mysticism and lack of worldly prudence), for his lofty aims and disinterested zeal for humanity. Two years later came Nathaniel Hawthorne, a mystic of a gloomier type, who brought his bride, Sophia Peabody, to the seclusion of the Old Manse which had been Dr. Ripley's residence. Hawthorne's sister-in-law, the talented Elizabeth Peabody, had already settled in Concord; and Margaret Fuller, the Zenobia of his famous romance, plain in her personal appearance as compared with that brilliant heroine, yet exercising no less marvellous fascination by her learn-

*"Died," a brief obituary for Anna Jones, was Thoreau's first known publication. It appeared in the Concord *Yeoman's Gazette* for November 25, 1837. See Walter Harding and Michael Meyer, *The New Thoreau Handbook* (New York: New York University Press, 1980), 34.—Eds.

†Emerson moved to Concord, into the Old Manse, in October 1834; he married Lydia Jackson in 1835 and moved, in September of that year, into the house on Lexington Road that was to be his home for the rest of his life. See Harding, *Days of Henry David Thoreau,* 60.—Eds.

ing, genius, versatility, and rich sympathetic nature, was a frequent visitor for weeks together in the village, where her sister, Ellen Fuller, who had married Ellery Channing, the poet, was then living. Here too resided Elizabeth Hoar, another of those thoughtful women by whom the Concord society was rendered remarkable.

These, with Henry Thoreau, were the chief members of that transcendentalist company of which Concord was the meeting place. As early as 1840 he was fully admitted into the inner circle of which Emerson, Alcott, and Margaret Fuller were the chief representatives, and he used to be present at Alcott's philosophical "conversations," held at Emerson's house, which were attended by many ardent thinkers from Boston, Cambridge, and other neighbouring towns.

Early in 1841 he was invited by Emerson to become an inmate of his household, and for two years from that time he lived under his friend's roof. "He is to have his board, etc., for what labour he chooses to do," wrote Emerson, "and he is thus far a great benefactor and physician to me, for he is an indefatigable and skilful labourer." Emerson's house was a square, substantial building on the Boston Road,* at the outskirts of the village. The ground was low-lying, and at first somewhat bare and open, but some fruit-trees were planted by Thoreau in which Emerson afterwards delighted. Emphatic testimony to Thoreau's helpfulness and kindness of heart has been borne by Emerson's son in his memoirs of his father.[5] "He was as little troublesome a member of the household, with his habits of plain living and high thinking, as could well have been, and in the constant absences of the master of the house in his lecturing trips, the presence there of such a friendly and sturdy inmate was a great comfort. He was handy with tools, and there was no limit to his usefulness and ingenuity about the house and garden." That Emerson at times felt a little out of sympathy with the rather pugnacious and contradictory temperament of his young friend, as shown in his suggestive remark, "Thoreau is, with difficulty, sweet," is probable enough, and does not necessarily conflict with the above statement.

Thoreau's friendship with Alcott, though less intimate than with Emerson, was very constant and sincere, and Alcott himself has borne grateful testimony to the worth of Thoreau as a friend. Margaret Fuller, whose connection with the *Dial* brought her into association and correspondence with Thoreau, also seems to have felt considerable interest in

*The house was on the Cambridge turnpike.—Eds.

his character at this time, and expressed herself in her letters with her wonted candour and freedom. In rejecting some verses which Thoreau had offered for publication, she thus sketches the outlines, as they appear to her, of his personality:—

> He is healthful, rare, of open eye, ready hand, and noble scope. He sets no limit to his life, nor to the invasions of nature; he is not wilfully pragmatical, cautious, ascetic, or fantastical. But he is as yet a somewhat bare hill, which the warm gales of spring have not visited. Yet what could a companion do at present, unless to tame the guardian of the Alps too early? Leave him at peace amid his native snows. He is friendly; he will find the generous office that shall educate him. It is not a soil for the citron and the rose, but for the whortleberry, the pine, or the heather.

In this same year Thoreau made another acquaintance which soon ripened into the warmest friendship of his life. Ellery Channing, the nephew of the great Unitarian minister, Dr. W. E. Channing, and the brother-in-law of Margaret Fuller, came to Concord in 1841, and lived for a time in a cottage near Emerson's house.* He was a poet and a man of genius, though of so whimsical, moody, and unstable a character that he never won the popularity which his friends were constantly anticipating for him. Between him and Thoreau, whose junior he was by one year,† there was quickly established a strong bond of sympathy and mutual understanding, which perhaps originated in the fact that each stood in a position of antagonism towards the canons of society. Channing, who was as impatient of routine as Thoreau himself, had not graduated at the University; and while his new friend had been keeping school at Concord he had been living in a log-hut in the wilds of Illinois. In his devotion to nature and natural scenery his tastes exactly coincided with Thoreau's, and many were the rambling walks and talks they had together at all hours and seasons, while the good folk of Concord were intent on their more sober business. "In our walks," says Thoreau, "Channing takes out his notebook sometimes and tries to write as I do, but all in vain. He soon puts it up again, or contents

*Ellery Channing and his wife, the former Ellen Fuller, settled in Concord in 1843.—Eds.

†Ellery Channing was born November 29, 1817.—Eds.

himself with scrawling some sketch of the landscape. He is the moodiest person, perhaps, that I ever saw."[6]

It was well for Henry Thoreau that at this period of his early manhood he had formed these lasting friendships with such men as Emerson, Alcott, and Channing; for a blow was impending which might otherwise have left him lonely and friendless on the very threshold of active life. We have seen how his natural self-control and fortitude of character enabled him to perform an act of self-renunciation for the sake of the brother to whom he was so closely attached; he was now to be subjected to a still severer trial by the unexpected death of the companion of his youthful days. On January 11th, 1842 John Thoreau died from lock-jaw, caused by an injury done to his hand in shaving—a death so sudden and painful that his brother could rarely endure to hear mention of it in after-life, and is said to have turned pale and faint when narrating the circumstances to a friend more than twelve years later. "After the sad and unfortunate death of his brother," says one who knew them both, "he seemed to have no earthly companion in whom he could confide and love; he appeared indifferent to all about him, and sometimes I thought he even hated himself."[7] Yet he could write thus in a letter of March 2, "I find these things more strange than sad to me. What right have I to grieve, who have not ceased to wonder? Only Nature has a right to grieve perpetually, for she only is innocent." It is noticeable that in his *Week on the Concord and Merrimac[k] Rivers,* his brother, though necessarily often alluded to, is not once mentioned by name.

For this heavy blow Thoreau sought and found the needed comfort in that strong belief in the immutable goodness of Nature, which was the basis of his whole intellectual creed. He had lost the loved companion of his daily pilgrimage; but one effect of his brother's death was to incline him still more strongly towards a close study of nature and the transcendental manner of thought; he might indeed have been in danger of lapsing into that vague mysticism which was the besetting weakness of some of the transcendentalists, had it not been for the sound practical frame of mind which was as much a part of him as his idealism. It was this solid element of good sense that kept the balance in his character; soar as he might in his transcendental reveries, and scoff as he might at the absurdities of conventional habit, he never lost hold on the simple essential facts of everyday life.

NOTES

1. This was the "Parkman" House, in the centre of the village, where the Public Library now stands. The Thoreaus lived in this house from 1837 to 1844; then in the "Texas" House, built by Henry's father, in a rather remoter quarter, till 1850.

2. "With regard to the private school of John and Henry Thoreau," says Dr. Edward Emerson (Centenary Edition of *Emerson's Writings, X,* 609) "I collected the testimony, some twenty years [ago], of such of the scholars as I could find, and all but one had remembered it as a privilege of their lives; they loved John and respected Henry" (1904).

3. Edmund Sewall died in the autumn of 1908. I am informed on good authority that when asked to whom the poem "Sympathy" was addressed, he replied, "I suppose it was to me." It is quite possible that this may have been the case, and that there may also have been an underlying reference to his sister. It has also been stated by Mr. C. H. Greene, on the authority of Sophia Thoreau, that the poem "Sympathy" referred to Thoreau's brother John. The reader must choose which interpretation he will, where none is wholly satisfactory.

4. Twelve years later Thoreau could write in his Journal (Nov. 14, 1851): "I confess that I am lacking a sense, perchance, in this respect, and I derive no pleasure from talking with a young woman half an hour simply because she has regular features. The society of young women is the most unprofitable I have ever tried." See, too, the letter to Emerson in which he refers to a certain "tragic correspondence" with an unnamed lady. "She did really wish to—I hesitate to write—marry me. That is the way they spell it." *Familiar Letters,* 138, 139.

5. *Emerson in Concord,* by Dr. E. W. Emerson. See also the Centenary *Emerson, X,* 606.

6. *Journal,* Nov. 8, 1851.

7. *Some Recollections and Incidents Concerning Thoreau,* by Joseph Hosmer.

3

Friendship with Emerson

After his brother's death in 1842 Thoreau continued to live in Emerson's house, the bereavement which each of the two friends had recently undergone—for little Waldo, Emerson's favourite child, had died early in the same year—being doubtless instrumental in bringing them more closely together.[1] Thoreau's regard for Emerson and Mrs. Emerson was very deep, and it was natural that a young man, even when possessed of his strength of character, should be lastingly influenced by so commanding a personality as Emerson's. It has been remarked by several of those who knew both men, that Thoreau unconsciously caught certain of the traits of Emerson's voice and expression, and even of his personal appearance—that he deliberately imitated Emerson is declared on the best authority to be an "idle and untenable" assertion. The following account of Thoreau's receptivity in this respect is given by one of his college class-mates, whom I have already quoted:—

> Not long after I happened to meet Thoreau in Mr. Emerson's study at Concord—the first time we had come together after leaving college. I was quite startled by the transformation that had taken place in him. His short figure and general cast of countenance were of course unchanged; but in his manners, in the tones of his voice, in his modes of expression, even in the hesitations and pauses of his speech, he had become the counterpart of Mr. Emerson. Thoreau's college voice bore no resemblance to Mr. Emerson's, and was so familiar to my ear that I could have readily

identified him by it in the dark. I was so much struck by the change that I took the opportunity, as they sat near together talking, of listening with closed eyes, and I was unable to determine with certainty which was speaking. I do not know to what subtle influences to ascribe it, but after conversing with Mr. Emerson for even a brief time, I always found myself able and inclined to adopt his voice and manner of speaking.[2]

The change noticed in Thoreau was not due only to the stimulating influence of Emerson's personality, though that doubtless was the immediate means of effecting his awakening. Underneath the sluggish and torpid demeanour of his life at the University there had been developing, as his school-mates afterwards recognised, the strong stern qualities which were destined to make his character remarkable, and these had now been called into full play both by the natural growth of his mind, and by the opportunities afforded in the brilliant circle of which he was a member. "In later years," says John Weiss, who knew him well at Harvard, "his chin and mouth grew firmer, as his resolute and audacious opinions developed, the eyes twinkled with the latent humour of his criticisms of society."[3]

So too with regard to his social and ethical opinions; it would have been strange if the youth of twenty-five had not been in some degree affected and influenced by the philosopher of forty; but the freshness and originality of his genius, in all essential respects, is none the less incontestable. Thoreau, in fact, was one of the very few men by whom Emerson was himself in some degree impressed. We are told by Dr. E. W. Emerson that his father "delighted in being led to the very inner shrines of the wood-god by this man, clear-eyed and true and stern enough to be trusted with their secrets;" and there is no doubt that Thoreau influenced him perceptibly in the direction of a more diligent and minute study of nature, and a simpler and austerer mode of life. He differed in one important respect both from Emerson and from the other members of the Emersonian circle of transcendentalists—in his aboriginal hardihood and vigour. To them Concord was a suitable place of adoption; to him it was the place of his birth. The simplicity of living, personal independence, and intimacy with wild nature, which to the others involved more or less a deliberate effort, were in his case an innate and unconscious instinct.

With Nathaniel Hawthorne, who was the latest addition to the society of Concord, Thoreau had perhaps little in common except his friendship with Ellery Channing, though courteous relations seem to have subsisted between them. Some of the references to Thoreau in Hawthorne's journal have a touch of the petulance and harshness of judgment to which Hawthorne was rather prone when recording his impressions of his acquaintances; but on the whole he speaks of Thoreau with unusual admiration and respect. "Mr. Thoreau dined with us yesterday," he writes on 1st September 1842. "He is a singular character—a young man with much of wild original nature still remaining in him; and so far as he is sophisticated, it is in a way and method of his own. He is as ugly as sin, long-nosed, queer-mouthed, and with uncouth and somewhat rustic though courteous manners corresponding very well with such an exterior. But his ugliness is of an honest and agreeable fashion, and becomes him much better than beauty." No reliance is to be placed in some further remarks of Hawthorne's, to the effect that Thoreau's sojourn in Emerson's household had been burdensome to his host, for all the facts point strongly in the other direction.

On another occasion we learn that Thoreau rowed Hawthorne on the Concord river in the boat built and used by himself and his brother in their week's excursion to the Merrimac[k] in 1839, and Hawthorne, delighted at Thoreau's skill in paddling, decided to purchase the boat and change its name from *Musketaquid* to *Pond-lily.*[4] But the art of managing a canoe, which Thoreau had learnt from some Indians who had visited Concord a few years previously, was not to be acquired in a day. "Mr. Thoreau had assured me," writes Hawthorne plaintively, "that it was only necessary to will the boat to go in any particular direction, and she would immediately take that course, as if imbued with the spirit of the steersman. It may be so with him, but it is certainly not so with me." The difficulty once mastered, Hawthorne took much pleasure in his new purchase, and seems to have been inspired by something of Thoreau's enthusiasm for the wildness of open-air life. "Oh that I could run wild," he exclaims, when recording his first successful voyage in the *Pond-lily;* "that is, that I could put myself in a true relation with nature, and be on friendly terms with all congenial elements."

By the middle of 1842 the *Dial,* which had never been prosperous from a pecuniary point of view, was in severe straits, and the editorship having been resigned by Margaret Fuller, was undertaken by Emerson himself, in which work he was largely assisted by Thoreau, who was then living in his house. It is said that Thoreau not only canvassed for new subscribers, read proof-sheets, and selected passages from the "Ethnical Scriptures" of the Oriental philosophers, which formed one of the features of the *Dial* under Emerson's management, but also acted as sole editor on one or two occasions during his friend's absence.[5] A large number of Thoreau's writings were inserted by Emerson, whose estimate of his ability was far higher than that held by Margaret Fuller; so that the young author was now becoming recognised as one of the leaders of transcendental thought. The *Dial* for July 1842 contained his delightful essay on "The Natural History of Massachusetts," to which Emerson prefixed an introductory note in which he hinted that Izaak Walton and White of Selborne had now a worthy successor. The "Winter Walk," another essay of the same character and of almost equal merit, appeared in the *Dial* a year later.

In July, 1842, Thoreau, accompanied by a friend, went on a three days' excursion to Wachusett, a mountain to the west of Concord ("the blue wall," he calls it, "which bounds the western horizon"), which, from its isolated position, forms a conspicuous feature in the landscape, and is familiar by name to all readers of his writings. More than once he expresses a feeling of sympathy with this solitary height—

> But special I remember thee,
> Wachusett, who like me
> Standest alone without society.

His love of solitude and indifference or dislike to "society," in the ordinary sense of the word, may be gathered from a good deal of what has already been related of him. There was an aloofness and reserve in his nature which, together with his stern and lofty ideals, made him appear at times somewhat unbending and unapproachable. It was no question of being better, or worse, than the generality of men—he was different; and the sympathy which he could not find in civilised man he sought in wild nature, though well aware that Nature herself is nothing except in her relation to man. "I feel," he said, "that my life is very homely, my pleasures very cheap. Joy and sorrow, success and failure, grandeur and meanness, and indeed most words in the English language, do not mean for me what they do for my neighbours. I see that my neighbours look with compassion on me, that they think it is a mean and unfortunate destiny which makes me to walk in these fields and woods so much, and sail on this river alone. But so long as I find here the only real Elysium, I cannot hesitate in my choice."

To say, as is often said, that Thoreau was unsocial is, however, incorrect, except in a limited and qualified degree. "He enjoyed common people," says Channing; "he relished strong acrid characters." The rough honest farmers of Concord were his especial favourites, and in their company he could show plenty of that good fellowship of which he appeared, under some conditions, to be deficient. The impression which he left on his friends in Emerson's household, after his two years' residence there, was a wholly agreeable one. "He was by no means unsocial," says Dr. E. W. Emerson, "but a kindly and affectionate person, especially to children, whom he could endlessly amuse and charm in most novel and healthful ways. With grown persons he had tact and high courtesy, though with reserve. But folly, or pretence, or cant, or subserviency, excited his formidable attack."

Early in 1843* Thoreau ceased to live in Emerson's house, having accepted the offer of a tutorship in the family of Judge Emerson, the brother of the Concord philosopher, who was then living in Staten Island, near New York. Before leaving Concord to take up this duty, he wrote as follows to Emerson, who was lecturing at New York, January 24, 1843:—

> At the end of this strange letter I will not write what alone I had to say—to thank you and Mrs. Emerson for your long kindness to me. It would be more ungrateful than my constant thought. I have been your pensioner for nearly two years, and still left free as under the sky. It has been as free a gift as the sun or the summer, though I have sometimes molested you with my mean acceptance of it—I, who have failed to render even those slight services of the *hand* which would have been for a sign at least; and, by the fault of my nature, have failed of many better and higher services. But I will trouble you no more with this, but for once thank you as well as Heaven.

It is probable that some stanzas of Thoreau's entitled "The Departure" were written about this time, when he had just left with regret the friends whose house had for two years been his home.

Several months were spent by Thoreau in Staten Island. Here, in his

*Thoreau left for Staten Island on May 6, 1843.—Eds.

spare hours during the spring and summer of 1843, he continued his walking excursions as regularly as at Concord, and was frequently mistaken by the inhabitants for a busy surveyor, who was studying every yard of the ground with a view to some extensive speculation. From an old ruined fort he used to watch the emigrant vessels pass up the narrow channel from the wide outer bay and go on their course to New York, or, as the case might be, remain in quarantine at Staten Island, when the passengers would be allowed to go ashore and refresh themselves on that "artificial piece of the land of liberty." From the low hills in the interior of the island, among the homesteads where the Huguenots had been the first settlers, he could see the long procession of out-going ships, stretching far as the eye could reach, "with stately march and silken sails," as he describes it; at other times he roamed along the desolate sandy shore, where packs of half-wild dogs were on the lookout for carcases of horses or oxen washed up by the tide. "An island," he says, in his *Week,* "always pleases my imagination, even the smallest, as a continent and integral portion of the globe. I have a fancy for building my hut on one. Even a bare, grassy isle, which I can see entirely over at a glance, has some undefined and mysterious charms for me."

It was at Staten Island that Thoreau wrote those beautiful and highly characteristic stanzas on the sea:—

My life is like a stroll upon the beach,
   As near the ocean's edge as I can go;
My tardy steps its waves sometimes o'erreach,
   Sometimes I stay to let them overflow.

My sole employment 'tis, and scrupulous care,
   To place my gains beyond the reach of tides,
Each smoother pebble, and each shell more rare,
   Which Ocean kindly to my hand confides.

I have but few companions on the shore:
   They scorn the strand who sail upon the sea;
Yet oft I think the ocean they've sailed o'er
   Is deeper known upon the strand to me.

The middle sea contains no crimson dulse,
   Its deeper waves cast up no pearls to view;
Along the shore my hand is on its pulse,
   And I converse with many a shipwrecked crew.

During the sojourn in Staten Island, Thoreau was frequently in New York, where he made the acquaintance of W. H. Channing, Edward Palmer, Lucretia Mott, Henry James, Horace Greeley, and other persons of note. "In this city," he wrote to his sister on 21st July, "I have seen, since I last wrote, W. H. Channing, at whose house in Fifteenth Street I spent a few pleasant hours, discussing the all-absorbing question—what to do for the race. Also Horace Greeley, editor of the *Tribune,* who is cheerfully in earnest at his office of all work, a hearty New Hampshire boy as one could wish to meet, and says, 'Now be neighbourly.'" With Greeley, who was at this time preaching Fourierism in the *New York Tribune,* in conjunction with Margaret Fuller and George Ripley, Thoreau established a firm friendship; and it will be seen that Greeley was able, a few years later, to render him valuable service in securing publication for his writings. In a letter addressed to Emerson from Staten Island, 23rd May 1843, Thoreau thus relates his impressions of New York:—

> You must not count much upon what I can do or learn in New York. Everything there disappoints me but the crowd, rather, I was disappointed with the rest before I came. I have no eyes for their churches, and what else they find to brag of. Though I know but little about Boston, yet what attracts me in a quiet way seems much meaner and more pretending than there—libraries, pictures, and faces in the street. You don't know where any respectability inhabits. The crowd is something new and to be attended to. It is worth a thousand Trinity Churches and Exchanges, while it is looking at them; and it will run over them and trample them underfoot one day. There are two things I hear and am aware I live in the neighbourhood of—the roar of the sea and the hum of the city.

Though literary work had not yet come to be regarded by Thoreau as his principal employment, his pen was not idle during his visit to Staten Island. He wrote some articles for the *Democratic Review* and *Dial,* and made some translations from the Greek of Æschylus and Pindar. The *Dial,* in spite of the fact that its contributors wrote gratuitously, was unable to pay its way, and the difficulties in which it was already involved led to its discontinuance in the spring of 1844. But although the transcendentalist organ thus failed to win the necessary public support, transcendentalism as a movement was now in the heyday of its vigour. It was, as we have seen, part of the creed that every one should labour with his own hands, and that men should endeavour to revert, as much as possible, from an artificial to a simple mode of living. When these thoughts began to be embodied in deeds the movement took two directions, the one towards collective action, and the other towards individualism. It was in reference to the former that Emerson wrote to Carlyle in 1840: "We are all a little wild with numberless projects of social reform; not a reading man but has a draft of a new community in his waistcoat pocket." The most important of such communal projects was the famous Brook Farm experiment, which was commenced in the spring of 1841, and came to an end in 1847, on which subject the opinion of the chief transcendentalists was divided, Margaret Fuller and George Ripley favouring the enterprise, while Emerson, Alcott, and Thoreau stood aloof. The spread of Fourierism in New England during these same years had led to the establishment of "Phalansteries," in which Horace Greeley and W. H. Channing took a leading part. Yet another attempt at colonisation was that made by Alcott and one or two friends in 1843, on an estate near Harvard, which was purchased by them and named "Fruitlands." This small colony, to which Thoreau paid a visit,* though he declined the offer of membership, was, like most of the rest, a failure; and in less than a year Alcott gave it up and returned to Concord.

Of the second, or individualist, method of practising the "return to nature," Thoreau himself was destined to be the most successful exponent. His utter distrust of communities is very characteristic of his independent and self-assertive temperament. "As for these communities," he wrote in his journal, "I think I had rather keep bachelor's hall in hell than go to board in heaven." But, though he had no intention of sacrificing one iota of his individuality by joining a community at Brook Farm or elsewhere, he had for some time been considering the feasibility of putting his principles into practice by a temporary and tentative withdrawal from the society of his fellow-townsmen, a plan which was possibly suggested to him by his friend Stearns Wheeler, who lived for some months, in 1841 or 1842, in a hut near Flint's Pond,

*According to Walter Harding, Thoreau was not even tempted to visit Fruitlands. See *The Days of Henry Thoreau,* 126.—Eds.

where he was visited by Thoreau.* This desire appears in his journal as early as 1841. "I want to go soon and live away by the pond," he wrote on December 24th, "where I shall hear only the wind whispering among the reeds. It will be success if I shall have left myself behind. But my friends ask what I will do when I get there. Will it not be employment enough to watch the progress of the seasons?" A couple of months before the date of this entry Margaret Fuller had written to Thoreau: "Let me know whether you go to the lonely hut, and write to me about Shakespeare if you read him there." It has already been mentioned that Walden Pond was associated with his earliest reminiscences; as a child he had thought he would like to live there, and as a boy he had been accustomed to come to its shores on dark nights, and fish for the "pouts" which were supposed to be attracted by the glare of a fire lit close to the water's edge, or, on a summer morning, to sit and muse for hours in his boat, as it drifted where the wind took it.

There was, however, another spot with which he was also familiar, which came very near being the scene of his projected hermitage. In his youthful voyages up the Concord river he had noticed, at a distance of about two miles from the village, an old-fashioned ruinous farm-house, concealed behind a dense grove of red maples, through which was heard the barking of the house-dog. This was the Hollowell Farm, the seclusion of which, if we may trust a passage in *Walden,* so tempted Thoreau that, at some period in his early manhood, he actually agreed to become its possessor. But before the purchase was effected and the contract signed, the owner of the place changed his mind, and had no difficulty in inducing Thoreau to release him from the bargain.

We may surmise that in 1844, after the conclusion of his educational engagement in Staten Island, he was still more decidedly bent on putting his favourite plan into execution; and that his thoughts now reverted to Walden woods as the place most suitable for his purpose.[6] Alcott's experiment at "Fruitlands," although unsuccessful in a pecuniary sense, had doubtless stimulated Thoreau's inclination to a forest life; and Emerson himself, while sceptical, in the main, as to the wisdom of such enterprises, had bought land on both sides of Walden Pond, with the idea of building a summer-house. Ellery Channing, who in his youth had made trial of a rough backwoods life, was of course taken into

*Wheeler lived at Flint's Pond in 1837.—Eds.

his friend's confidences respecting this retirement to the woods. "I see nothing for you in this earth," he wrote in 1845, "but that field which I once christened 'Briars'; go out upon that, build yourself a hut, and there begin the grand process of devouring yourself alive. I see no alternative, no other hope for you. Eat yourself up; you will eat nobody else, nor anything else."

Encouraged by these exhortations, and firmly trusting the promptings of his own destiny, Thoreau determined in the spring of 1845, being now in his twenty-eighth year, to build himself a hut on the shore of Walden Pond and there live for such time, and in such a manner, as might best conduce to his intellectual and spiritual advantage. The objects of his retirement have been so often misunderstood that they will bear repetition in his own words:—

> Finding that my fellow-citizens were not likely to offer me any room in the court-house, or any curacy or living anywhere else, but that I must shift for myself, I turned my face more exclusively than ever towards the woods, where I was better known. I determined to go into business at once, and not wait to acquire the usual capital, using such slender means as I had already got. My purpose in going to Walden Pond was not to live cheaply nor to live dearly there, but to transact some private business with the fewest obstacles. . . . I went to the woods because I wished to live deliberately, to front only the essential facts of life, and see if I could not learn what it had to teach, and not, when I came to die, discover that I had not lived. I did not wish to live what was not life, living is so dear; nor did I wish to practise resignation unless it was quite necessary. I wanted to live deep and suck out all the marrow of life, to live so sturdily and Spartan-like as to put to rout all that was not life, to cut a broad swath and shave close, to drive life into a corner, and reduce it to its lowest terms, and if it proved to be mean, why then to get the whole and genuine meanness of it, and publish its meanness to the world; or if it were sublime, to know it by experience, and be able to give a true account of it in my next excursion.

Walden was, in fact, to Thoreau what Brook Farm was to others of the transcendentalists—a retreat suitable for philosophic meditation, and the practice of a simpler, hardier, and healthier life.

NOTES

1. John Thoreau had also been intimate with Emerson's family, and it was by his arrangement that a portrait was taken of Waldo a few months before the child's death.

2. *Ralph Waldo Emerson,* by Rev. D. G. Haskins.

3. It has been suggested that the "transformation" of Donatello in Hawthorne's novel may have been founded in the first place on this fact in the life of Thoreau.

4. The boat is referred to in the Introduction to *Mosses from an Old Manse.* It was bequeathed by Hawthorne to Channing, who kept it till it fell to pieces.

5. Vol. iii., No. 3, is said to have been edited by Thoreau.

6. As throwing light on Thoreau's state of mind at this time, see his correspondence with Isaac Hecker (*Familiar Letters,* 404–408), a friend who had invited him to travel through Europe on foot and without money. "I am really sorry," he wrote, "that the genius will not let me go with you, but I trust that it will conduct to other adventures."

4

At Walden

Walden Pond, on the shore of which Thoreau determined to make his hermitage, is a small lake, about a mile and a half south of the village of Concord, surrounded by low thickly-wooded hills. Its water, which is of a greenish-blue colour, is so brilliantly transparent that the bottom is visible at a depth of thirty feet, in which respect it is unrivalled by the other ponds of the neighbourhood, except by White Pond, which lies some two miles westward, on the other side of the Concord river. Walden had in primitive ages been frequented by the Indians, as testified by arrow-heads discoverable on its shores, and by dim traces of a narrow shelf-like path, "worn by the feet of aboriginal hunters," which ran round the steeply-sloping bank. In the early days of the Massachusetts colony, the dense woods, which even in Thoreau's memory completely surrounded the pond, had been the haunt of fugitives and outlaws; but, at a later period, the road from Concord to Lincoln, which skirts the east shore of Walden, had been dotted by the cottages and gardens of a small hamlet, and had resounded, as Thoreau tells us, "with the laugh and gossip of inhabitants." Drink had been the ruin of these former settlers; and the hardy water-drinker who now came to make his home in Walden woods took care to choose a new and unpolluted spot for his dwelling.

The ground chosen by Thoreau for the building of his hut was on a wood-lot belonging to Emerson—a sloping bank at the outskirts of the forest, on the north shore of the pond, and some thirty or forty yards from the water-edge. No house could be seen from this point, the horizon being bounded by the woods on the opposite shore, half a mile distant; and although the village was within easy reach, and the newly-constructed railway was visible on one hand, and the woodland road on the other, there was no neighbour within a mile, and the solitude was usually as complete as the strictest anchorite could have desired. This position exactly suited Thoreau's requirements, since he could either pursue his meditations undisturbed, or, if the mood took him, pay a visit to his friends in the village, from whose society he had no intention of permanently banishing himself.

So one morning towards the end of March 1845, when the approach of spring was already heralded by the voice of song-birds and the thawing of the ice on Walden, the "Bachelor of Nature" addressed himself to the pleasurable task of "squatting" on the selected spot. Having borrowed the favourite axe of his friend Alcott, who warned him that it was "the apple of his eye," he began to cut down pine-trees and hew the timber into shape for the frame of his hut, working leisurely each day, so as to get the full enjoyment of his occupation, and returning betimes to the village to sleep. After two or three weeks spent in this labour, when the house was framed and ready for raising, he dug his cellar in the sand of the sloping bank, six feet square by seven deep; and having bought the planks of a shanty belonging to an Irishman who worked on the Fitchburg railroad, he transported them to the site of the hut. Early in May he set up the frame of his house, on which occasion—for the sake of neighbourliness, as he is careful to tell us, rather than of necessity—he accepted the assistance of some of his friends, among whom were Alcott (to whom he returned the axe sharper than he had received it), George William Curtis,[1] who was then spending a year or two at Concord, having hired himself out as an agricultural labourer, and Edmund Hosmer, one of the leading farmers of Concord, with whom Thoreau was on intimate terms. The hut, which was ten feet wide by fifteen feet long, with a garret and a closet, a large window at the side, a door at one end, and a brick fireplace at the other, was then boarded and roofed so as to be quite rain-proof, but during the summer months it remained without plastering or chimney. It was the 4th of July, or Independence Day—a significant and auspicious date for the commencement of such an undertaking—when Thoreau, who previously had been owner of no habitations but a boat and a tent, took up his residence in this house, which he could call his own property, and which, as he proudly records, had cost him but twenty-eight dollars in the building.

The question of "furnishing," which is a cause of such anxious consideration to so many worthy householders, was solved by Thoreau with his usual boldness and expedition. "Furniture!" he exclaims, in an outburst of pitying wonder at the spectacle of men who are enslaved by their own chattels. "Thank God, I can sit and I can stand without the aid of a furniture warehouse." His furniture at Walden, which was partly of his own manufacture, consisted of a bed, a table, a desk, three chairs, a looking-glass three inches in diameter, a pair of tongs and andirons, a kettle, a skillet, and a frying-pan, a dipper, a wash-bowl, two knives and forks, three plates, one cup, one spoon, a jug for oil, a jug for molasses, and a japanned lamp. Curtains he did not need, since there were no gazers to look in on him except the sun and moon, and he had no carpet in danger of fading, nor meat and milk to be guarded from sunshine or moonbeam. When a lady offered him a mat, he declined it as being too cumbrous and troublesome an article; he preferred to wipe his feet on the sod outside his door. Finding that three pieces of limestone which lay upon his desk required to be dusted daily, he threw them out of the window, determined that if he had any furniture to dust, it should be "the furniture of his mind." With a house thus organised, housework, instead of being an exhausting and ever-recurring labour, was a pleasant pastime.

> When my floor was dirty I rose early, and setting all my furniture out of doors on the grass, bed and bedstead making but one budget, dashed water on the floor, and sprinkled white sand from the pond on it, and then with a broom scrubbed it clean and white; and by the time the villagers had broken their fast, the morning sun had dried my house sufficiently to allow me to move in again, and my meditations were almost uninterrupted. It was pleasant to see my whole household effects on the grass, making a little pile like a gipsy's pack, and my three-legged table, from which I did not remove the books and pen and ink, standing amidst the pines and hickories.

Having thus chosen his surroundings, he was free to choose also the most congenial manner of life. He rose early, and took his bath in the pond, a habit which he regarded as nothing less than "a religious exercise." After the morning bath came the work—or the leisure—of the day. In the early summer, before the building was finished, he had ploughed and planted about two and a half acres of the light sandy soil in the neighbourhood of his hut, the crop chiefly consisting of beans, with a few potatoes, peas, and turnips; and during this first summer at Walden the bean-field was the chief scene of his labours, from five o'clock till noon being the hours devoted to the work. Day after day the travellers on the road from Concord to Lincoln would rein in their horses and pause to look with wonder on this strange husbandman, who cultivated a field where all else was wild upland, who put no manure on the soil, and continued to sow beans at a time when others had begun to hoe.[2]

Meantime the husbandman himself was deriving from his rough matter-of-fact occupation a sort of sublime transcendental satisfaction; it was agriculture and mysticism combined to which he was devoting his bodily and mental energies. What matter if, when the pecuniary gains and losses of the season came to be estimated, he found himself with a balance of but eight dollars in his favour, which represented his year's income from the farm? Was he not less anxious and more contented than his fellow-agriculturists of the village? The following season he improved on these results by cultivating only a third of an acre, and using the spade instead of the plough. Whatever money was further needed for his food and personal expenses, he earned by occasional day-labour in the village, for he had, as he tells us, "as many trades as fingers."

After a morning thus spent in work, whether manual or literary, he would refresh himself by a second plunge in the pond, and enjoy an afternoon of perfect freedom, rambling, according to his wont, by river or forest, wherever his inclination led him. He had also his entire days of leisure, when he could not afford "to sacrifice the bloom of the present moment to any work, whether of the head or hands." "Sometimes," he says, "in a summer morning, having taken my accustomed bath, I sat in my sunny doorway from sunrise till noon, rapt in a reverie, amidst the pines, and hickories, and sumachs, in undisturbed solitude and stillness, while the birds sang around or flitted noiseless through the house, until by the sun falling in at my west window, or the noise of some traveller's waggon on the distant highway, I was reminded of the lapse of time." He was well aware that these day-dreams must be accounted sheer idleness by his enterprising townsmen; but of that he himself was the best and only judge. On moonlit evenings he would walk on the sandy beach of the pond, and wake the echoes of the surrounding woods with his flute.

We may assume, too, that it was at this period, especially, that he felt those spiritual awakenings, and saw those inner visions, referred to in his poem "Inspiration":—

> But now there comes unsought, unseen,
> Some clear divine electuary,
> And I, who had but sensual been,
> Grow sensible, and as God is, am wary.
>
> I hearing get, who had but ears,
> And sight, who had but eyes before;
> I moments live, who lived but years,
> And truth discern, who knew but learning's lore.
>
> I hear beyond the range of sound,
> I see beyond the range of sight,
> New earths and skies and seas around,
> And in my day the sun doth pale his light.

We have seen what amount of shelter Thoreau thought needful for his comfort; his estimate of what is necessary in the way of food and clothing was conceived in the same spirit. His costume was habitually coarse, shabby, and serviceable; he would wear corduroy, Channing tells us, but not shoddy. His drab hat, battered and weatherstained, his clothes often torn and as often mended, his dusty cow-hide boots, all told of hard service in field and forest, and of the unwillingness of their wearer to waste a single dollar on the vanities of outward appearance. He wished his garments to become assimilated to himself, and to receive a true impress of his character; he would not be, like some king or nobleman, a wooden horse on which clean clothes might be hung for a day's ornament. His diet was fully as simple and economical as his clothing; his food, while he stayed at Walden, consisted of rice, Indian meal, potatoes, and very rarely salt pork, and his drink was water. He baked his own bread of rye and Indian meal, at first procuring yeast from the village, but afterwards coming to the conclusion that it was "simpler and more respectable" to omit it. He had a strong preference at all times for a vegetarian diet, though he would occasionally catch a mess of fish for his dinner from Walden Pond, and pleads guilty on one occasion to having slaughtered and devoured a wood-chuck which had made inroads on his bean field.

Here is an anecdote of Thoreau, to be taken for what it is worth:

One of the axioms of his philosophy had been to take the life of nothing that breathed, if he could avoid it; but it had now become a serious question with him whether to allow the wood-chucks and rabbits to destroy his beans, or to fight. Having determined on the latter, he procured a steel trap, and soon caught a venerable old fellow "to the manor born," and who had held undisputed possession there for all time. After retaining the enemy of all beans "in durance vile" for a few hours, he pressed his foot on the spring of the trap and let him go—expecting and hoping never to see him more. Vain delusion!

A few days after, on returning from the village post-office and looking in the direction of his bean-field, to his disgust and apprehension he saw the same old grey-back disappear behind some brush just outside the field. Accordingly he set the trap and again caught the thief.

Now it so happened that those old knights of the shot-gun, hook and line, Wesson, Pratt and Co., were on a piscatorial visit to the Pond. A council of war was thereupon held to determine what should be done with the wood-chuck.

A decision was rendered immediately by the landlord of the Middlesex Hotel in his terse and laconic manner: "Knock his brains out!"

This, however, was altogether too severe on the wood-chuck, thought Henry; even wood-chucks had some rights that "Squatter Sovereigns" should respect. Was he not the original occupant there; and had not *he* "jumped" the wood-chuck's "claim," destroyed his home and built the "hut" upon the ruins?

After considering the question carefully he took the wood-chuck in his arms and carried him some two miles away, and then, with a severe admonition at the end of a good stick, he opened the trap and again let him depart in peace,—and he never saw him more.[3]

In November, when the summer weather was ended and frost coming on apace, he put the finishing touches to his house by shingling its sides, building a fire-place and chimney, and finally plastering the walls. Hardly was this last process over when the winter set in with full severity, and by the middle of December the pond was completely frozen and the ground covered with snow. He now began, in the full sense, to inhabit his hermitage, his outdoor employments being limited to collecting and chopping firewood, while during the long evening hours he occupied himself with the journal, which he still kept with unfailing regularity, and which formed the basis of his *Walden* and the *Week on the Concord and Merrimac{k} Rivers,* the latter of which was now in course of preparation. Now, too, he had full leisure to weigh the respective merits of society and solitude. Of the solitude thus offered him he availed himself with gratitude and profit; it was during this period that he matured his thoughts and perfected his literary style, so that having come to Walden with still somewhat of the crudeness of youth, he might leave it with the firmness and dignity of manhood.

It is, however, a mistake to suppose that Thoreau was isolated from society during his seclusion at Walden—such had never been his intention, and such was not, in fact, the case. Every day or two, in winter as well as in summer, he strolled to the village to see his relatives and friends, and to hear the gossip of the hour, sometimes returning late at night after supper at a friend's house, and steering his way almost unconsciously through the darkness of the Walden woods. The Fitchburg railroad often provided him with a pathway on these occasions; indeed, so well known was he along the line, that the drivers of the trains were accustomed to bow to him as to an old acquaintance. Nor was the visiting altogether on Thoreau's side; for, as may well be believed, the news of his strange retirement brought him numerous unbidden guests, whom he received with such hospitality as was possible in his sylvan abode. To the simple holiday folk, who came to enjoy themselves and make the best of their time, such as children and railroad men, wood-choppers, fishermen, hunters, and even idiots from the almshouse, he seems invariably to have extended a hearty welcome and good fellowship; not so, perhaps, to the dilettante reformers, prying gossips, and sham philanthropists, whose advances he characteristically resented, men who "did not know when their visit had terminated," though he sought to indicate this fact to them by going about his business again, and answering them "from greater and greater remoteness."

He also received welcome visits from Emerson, on whose land he was "squatting," and from his other personal friends. Ellery Channing spent a fortnight with him in his hut at Walden, at the time when he was building his fireplace, and was a frequent visitor at all seasons of the year. Alcott was another of his regular guests, and it is he who is referred to in the pages of *Walden* as "one of the last of the philosophers," the man "of the most faith of any alive." On a Sunday afternoon he would sometimes be cheered by the approach of the "long-headed farmer," Edmund Hosmer, one of the firmest and heartiest of his friends, and the talk would then be of "rude and simple times, when men sat about large fires in cold bracing weather, with clear heads."

The following is a record of a visit paid to Thoreau by Joseph Hosmer, a kinsman of his farmer friend:—

> Early in September 1845, on his invitation, I spent a Sunday at his lake-side retreat. His hospitality and manner of entertainment were unique, and peculiar to the time and place. The cooking apparatus was primitive, and consisted of a hole made in the earth and inlaid with stones, upon which the fire was made, after the manner at the sea-shore when they have a clam-bake. When sufficiently hot, remove the embers and place on the fish, frog, etc.
>
> Our bill-of-fare included horned pout, corn, bread, beans, salt, etc. The beans had been previously cooked. The meal for our bread was mixed with lake water only, and when prepared it was spread upon the surface of a thin stone used for that purpose, and baked. When the bread had been sufficiently baked the stone was removed, then the fish was placed over the hot stones and roasted—some in wet paper and some without—and when seasoned with salt they were delicious.

It will be seen from these instances that Thoreau was by no means the misanthrope that some have imagined him. He well knew the value of social intercourse; but, on the other hand, he knew also that "society is commonly too cheap"; he loved at times to be alone, and confesses that he "never found the companion that was so companionable as solitude." His hut, as Channing has remarked, "was only a larger coat and hat to him, a garment he had left down by Walden, convenient to walk into if it rained."

It has been supposed that the Walden hermitage was occasionally a refuge to quite other visitors than those who have been enumerated, and that Thoreau's hut was a station in the great "Underground Railway" for runaway slaves; I am informed, however, on good authority, that this is an error. "I have made this a matter of special investigation," says Dr. S. A. Jones,[4] "and the truth is that there were specially prepared houses in 'Old Concord' which afforded infinitely more secure resting and hiding-places for the fugitive slave. Moreover, the survivors who managed Concord 'station' declare that Thoreau's hut was not used for such a purpose."

It was in connection with Thoreau's abolitionist enthusiasm that a remarkable incident befell him during his first autumn at Walden. His individualistic view of life had naturally led him, as it led Alcott and some other transcendentalists, to the adoption of anarchist doctrines, and he heartily accepted and endorsed the dictum that "that government is best which governs not at all." His deep disapproval of the foreign policy of the United States in their war with Mexico, and his still stronger detestation of the sanction given by Government to negro slavery at home, had the effect of spurring his latent discontent into a sense of active personal antagonism to the State and its representatives, and he felt that something more than a verbal protest was demanded from those who, like himself, were required to show their allegiance in the form of taxes. "I meet this American Government, or its representative the State Government, directly, and face to face, once a year—no more—in the person of its tax-gatherer. . . . If a thousand men were not to pay their tax-bills this year, that would not be a violent and bloody measure, as it would be to pay them, and enable the State to commit violence and shed innocent blood."[5]

The first difficulty of this kind had arisen in 1843, when Alcott, who was probably acting in conjunction with Thoreau, was arrested for his refusal to pay the tax; but it was not till 1845[6]* that the State proceeded against the younger and, as it was presumably thought, less important offender. So when his "civil neighbour," Sam Staples, the tax-gatherer, came to Thoreau for the poll-tax,[7] it was refused (as the church-tax had been refused by him in 1838) on the ground that he did not care to trace the course of his dollar "till it buys a man, or a musket to shoot one with." One afternoon, when he chanced to have gone in from Walden to the village to get a shoe from the cobbler's, he was intercepted by Staples, who said that if he did not pay he would have to lock him up soon. "As well now as any time," was the reply, so with a "Well, come along then," Staples lodged him in the town gaol. "Henry, why are you here?" were the words of Emerson, when he came to visit his friend in this new place of retirement. "Why are you *not* here?" was the signifi-

*Thoreau went to jail during the summer of 1846, not 1845.—Eds.

cant reply of the prisoner, in allusion to the characteristic caution of Emerson.

A humorous account of the night he spent in prison, and of the fellow-criminals he met there, was afterwards written by Thoreau. "It was like travelling," he tells us, "into a far country, such as I had never expected to behold, to lie there for one night. It seemed to me that I had never heard the town-clock strike before, nor the evening sounds of the village, for we slept with the windows open, which were inside the grating. It was a closer view of my native town. I was fairly inside of it. I never had seen its institutions before. I began to comprehend what its inhabitants were about." The next morning he was discharged, his mother and aunts having paid the tax without his consent—a somewhat tame conclusion of the dispute on which he had not reckoned.[8] He proceeded straight from the prison door, among the meaning glances of his fellow-townsmen, to finish the errand in which he had been interrupted overnight, and having put on his mended shoe, was soon in command of a huckleberry party, on a hill two miles from Concord, from which spot, as he characteristically remarked, "the State was nowhere to be seen."

During all his walks over the fields and forests of the Walden neighbourhood, in which he was absent for hours, and sometimes days together, he never fastened the door of his hut; yet he never missed anything but a volume of Homer, and "was never molested by any person but those who represented the State." His longest absence from Walden seems to have been the fortnight he spent in Maine, in September 1846, when, in company with a cousin who was residing at Bangor, he explored the recesses of the Maine woods, ascended the mountain Ktaadn, and made acquaintance with some of the native Indian hunters, whose habits he was never weary of studying.

In 1847 he had some correspondence and personal intercourse with Agassiz, who had come to the States in the preceding autumn, and paid more than one visit to Concord. On several occasions collections of fishes, turtles, and various local *fauna* were sent to Agassiz by Thoreau, of whose knowledge and observation the great naturalist formed a high opinion. In one way, however, Thoreau differed widely from other members of the same profession, for, though a naturalist, he had discarded the use of the gun and the trap before he lived in the woods, his field-glass being the sole weapon of attack which he now carried in his excursions. Fishing was the only sport which he did not abandon, and even on this point his conscience was already uneasy, and he had discovered that he could not fish "without falling a little in self-respect."

Thus two summers and two winters passed by, fruitful in quiet meditation and ripening experience, though offering few incidents which call for special remark. When the summer of 1847 had arrived, he began to feel that the object for which he retired to Walden was now sufficiently accomplished, and that it was time for him to return to the more social atmosphere of the village. His period of retirement had not been wasted or misspent, for he had learnt by his experiment two great lessons concerning the practical life and the spiritual. First, "that to maintain one's self on this earth is not a hardship but a pastime, if we will live simply and wisely," it being his own experience that he could meet all the expenses of the year by six weeks of work. Secondly, "that if one advances confidently in the direction of his dreams, and endeavours to live the life which he has imagined, he will meet with a success unexpected in common hours; in proportion as he simplifies his life the laws of the universe will appear less complex, and solitude will not be solitude, nor poverty poverty nor weakness weakness." He had put his transcendental philosophy to the test, and the result had not disappointed him; he was no longer the "parcel of vain strivings" which he had pictured himself in his youthful poem, but he had now firm ground beneath his feet, and a clear object towards which to direct his course in the future.

On 6th September 1847 he left Walden, and again took up his residence in his father's household at Concord.[9] "I left the woods," he says, "for as good a reason as I went there. Perhaps it seemed to me that I had several more lives to live, and could not spare any more time for that one." "Why did I leave the woods?" he wrote in his journal a few years later. "I do not think that I can tell. I do not know any better how I came to go there. I have often wished myself back. Perhaps I wanted change. There was a little stagnation, it may be, about two o'clock in the afternoon. Perhaps if I lived there much longer, I might live there for ever. One might think twice before he accepted heaven on such terms."

Walden, the most famous of Thoreau's volumes, which contains the account of his life in the woods, was not published till 1854. That this most characteristic episode of his life should be a cause of wonder and misunderstanding to the majority of his readers and fellow-citizens, was, perhaps, only to be expected. Mention is made in one of the later diaries of an acquaintance of Emerson's, who was much interested in *Walden,* but who was convinced that the book was nothing more than a satire and *jeu d'esprit,* written solely for the amusement of the passing moment,—a misconception of the whole spirit of Thoreau's life, which is scarcely more wide of the mark than are some of the judgments passed on the Walden experiment in more recent criticism. "His shanty life," says Lowell, "was a mere impossibility, so far as his own conception of it goes, as an entire independency of mankind. The tub of Diogenes had a sounder bottom." But there is not a word to indicate that Thoreau was thinking of an "entire independency of mankind," or of abjuring a single product of civilisation which is of real use to men. The fact that this enterprise of Thoreau's, as described in his *Walden,* has been an encouragement and help to many persons, both in America and England, to live a simpler and saner life, is of itself sufficient testimony to the success of his endeavours. Yet Lowell's most unjustifiable confusion of simplicity with barbarism has again and again been quoted by later critics as an exposure of Thoreau's fallacies!

"Thoreau," says Dr. E. W. Emerson, "is absurdly misconceived by most people. He did not wish that every one should live in isolated cabins in the woods, on Indian corn and beans and cranberries. His own Walden camping was but a short experimental episode, and even then this really very human and affectionate man constantly visited his friends in the village, and was a most dutiful son and affectionate brother. It is idle for cavilling Epicureans to announce as a great discovery that he sometimes took supper comfortably at a friend's house, or was too good a son to churlishly thumb back the cake that his good mother had specially made for him." To the same misunderstanding of Thoreau's motives must be traced the foolish stories that are sometimes told of his receiving dainties from visitors, or listening for Emerson's dinner-bell.

It is necessary, if we would understand Thoreau aright, to appreciate carefully the importance of his sojourn at Walden in relation to the rest of his career. It seems to be sometimes forgotten that the period of his retirement was only two years out of the twenty of his adult life, and that it is therefore an injustice to him to connect his work too exclusively with Walden, or to speak of that episode as containing the sum and substance of his philosophical belief. It was a time of self-probation rather than an attempt to influence others, a trial rather than an expression of his transcendental ideas; he was under thirty years of age when he went to Walden, had published no volumes, and was altogether unknown except to a limited circle of his fellow-townsmen. On the other hand, it must be noted that this was the time when his thoughts ripened, and his ethical creed assumed a definite form, and that his residence in the woods was not only the most striking, because the most picturesque, incident in his life, but also gave a determining direction to his later career. He was a student when he came to Walden; when he returned to Concord he was a teacher.

And now, at this critical point in Thoreau's story, it may be well to interrupt for a time the external narrative of his life, in order to show what manner of man he was, in appearance, character, sympathies, studies, and other personal traits, when he thus came forward to preach to an inattentive world his gospel of simplicity.

NOTES

1. In his contribution to *Homes of American Authors* he refers to Thoreau's hut. "One pleasant afternoon a small party of us helped him raise it—a bit of life as Arcadian as any at Brook Farm."

2. Some pines afterwards planted by Thoreau on his bean-field were destroyed by fire May 18, 1896.

3. *Some Recollections and Incidents concerning Thoreau,* by Joseph Hosmer.

4. *Lippincott's Magazine,* August 1891. In the first edition of this book I was in error on this point.

5. Essay on *Civil Disobedience,* 1849.

6. The date is wrongly given in Emerson's Memoir as 1847.

7. Sam Staples, tax-gatherer, constable, and jailer in one, was a character in Concord, and there are some racy references to him in the *Journals.* Thoreau describes him as "quick, clear, downright, and on the whole a good fellow."

8. The payment of the tax has been wrongly ascribed to Emerson. The money was actually handed to the gaoler by Miss Maria Thoreau, disguised by wrapping something round her head. Nearly fifty years later Staples told an inquirer that the payment made Thoreau "mad as the devil."

9. The hut in which he had spent so many pleasant hours was bought a few years later by a farmer, and removed to another quarter of the Concord township, where it was used as a small granary and tool-house till it fell to pieces in 1868, having lasted twenty-three years. The sketch of the hut, most commonly engraved, was by Sophia Thoreau.

5

Personality

The personality of Thoreau was one which seldom failed to arrest the attention of those who met him. "He was short of stature," says Mr. Moncure Conway, who visited him a few years after he left Walden, "well built, and such a man as I have fancied Julius Caesar to have been. Every movement was full of courage and repose; the tones of his voice were those of Truth herself; and there was in his eye the pure bright blue of the New England sky, as there was sunshine in his flaxen hair. He had a particularly strong aquiline Roman nose, which somehow reminded me of the prow of a ship." This description is fully corroborated by that given in *Thoreau, the Poet-Naturalist,* by Ellery Channing, who, from his long and intimate acquaintance with Thoreau, could speak with peculiar authority:—

> His face, once seen, could not be forgotten. The features were quite marked: the nose aquiline, or very Roman, like one of the portraits of Caesar (more like a beak, as was said); large overhanging brows above the deepest-set blue eyes that could be seen, in certain lights, and in others grey—eyes expressive of all shades of feeling, but never weak or near-sighted; the forehead not unusually broad or high, full of concentrated energy or purpose; the mouth with prominent lips, pursed up with meaning and thought when silent, and giving out when open a stream of the most varied and unusual and instructive sayings. His whole figure had an active earnestness, as if he had no moment to waste. Even

in the boat he had a wary, transitory air, his eyes on the outlook—perhaps there might be ducks, or the Blondin turtle, or an otter, or sparrow.

From 1840 to 1860 Thoreau's figure must have been a very familiar one to his fellow-townsmen of Concord, since he was abroad in all weathers and at all hours, a noticeable man with his sloping shoulders, "his eyes bent on the ground, his long swinging gait, his hands perhaps clasped behind him, or held closely at his side, the fingers made into a fist." The indomitable spirit that animated his whole character was written unmistakably in his personal appearance. "How deep and clear is the mark that thought sets upon a man's face!" was the exclamation of one who saw him for the first time.[1]

The homeliness of Thoreau's mode of dress has already been noticed, and this, during his more lengthy walks or excursions, often led to strange errors as to his object and vocation. In Cape Cod and elsewhere he was several times mistaken for a pedlar, and on board a steamboat on the Hudson river he was once asked for a "chaw o' baccy" by a by-stander, who took him for a shipmate. It is said that his speech "had always a *burr* in it," owing to his peculiar pronunciation of the letter *r;* but all his oddities of appearance and manner were soon forgotten under the singular charm of his conversation, the power of which is attested by all who knew him. He himself says, in a passage of his diary, that his *bon-mots* were the "ripe, dry fruit of long past experience," which fell from him easily without giving him either pain or pleasure. This experience was not gathered, as is usually the case, by foreign travel or a varied manner of life, but by shrewd native sense and keen practical insight. There was a wonderful fitness, Emerson tells us, between his body and mind. He was expert as a walker, swimmer, runner, rower, and in all outdoor employments;[2] he could measure any given distance or height by foot or eye with extraordinary precision, could estimate the exact weight of anything put into his hands, and from a box containing a bushel or more of loose pencils could take up just a dozen pencils at every grasp.

In 1847, in answer to a circular which was issued at the time for the purpose of collecting facts in the lives of the Harvard class of 1837, Thoreau wrote the following highly characteristic letter:—

> Am not married. I don't know whether mine is a profession, or a trade, or what not. It is not yet learned, and in every instance has

been practised before being studied. The mercantile part of it was begun by myself alone. It is not one but legion. I will give you some of the monster's heads. I am a Schoolmaster, a private Tutor, a Surveyor, a Gardener, a Farmer, a Painter (I mean a House Painter), a Carpenter, a Mason, a Day-labourer, a Pencil-maker, a Glass-paper-maker, a Writer, and sometimes a Poetaster. If you will act the part of Iolus, and apply a hot iron to any of these heads, I shall be greatly obliged to you. My present employment is to answer such orders as may be expected from so general an advertisement as the above. That is, if I see fit, which is not always the case, for I have found out a way to live without what is commonly called employment or industry, attractive or otherwise. Indeed, my steadiest employment, if such it can be called, is to keep myself at the top of my condition, and ready for whatever may turn up in heaven or on earth. The last two or three years I lived in Concord woods, alone, something more than a mile from any neighbour, in a house built entirely by myself.

P. S.—I beg that the class will not consider me an object of charity, and if any of them are in want of any pecuniary assistance and will make known their case to me, I will engage to give them some advice of more worth than money.[3]

He has sometimes been called an ascetic; but if he seldom used flesh or wine, tea or coffee, and other supposed "necessaries" of diet, this abstinence was assuredly due to the fact that he found he thus increased, rather than diminished, the pleasure of existence. "There is Thoreau," said his friend Channing. "Give him sunshine, and a handful of nuts, and he has enough." The rare delicacy of his nature showed itself in his abhorrence of every form of sensuality or grossness, and in his expressed desire to live "as tenderly and daintily as one would pluck a flower." Yet seldom has there been a greater lover of healthy physical life. The keenness of his senses was extraordinary, and the perceptions of colour, sound, smell, and taste are always spoken of in his diaries as luxuries for which he can never be sufficiently grateful. Music had at all times a peculiar attraction for him (he was himself a skilful player on the flute), and is repeatedly mentioned in the diaries and letters as one of the supreme delights of life.

It was perhaps his very insistence on the ideal that gave to his character a certain external coldness and remoteness. "I love Henry," said one of his friends,[4] "but I cannot like him; and as for taking his arm, I should as soon think of taking the arm of an elm-tree." The misunderstandings thus generated were keenly felt by Thoreau himself, who rightly attributes them to his own extreme sensibility and exacting disposition. There are a number of passages in the diaries in which his over-sensitive nature seems to be tormented by unnecessary doubts as to his relations with his friends; but Ellery Channing, who, as Thoreau's most intimate companion, should be an authority on this point, asserts positively that the essay on Friendship was "poetical and romantic," and that to read it literally would be to accuse its author of stupidity. "The living actual friendship and affection," says Channing, "which makes time a reality, no one knew better. He meant friendship, and meant nothing else, and stood by it without the slightest abatement."

To a man of this temperament, who needed leisure, breathing-space, and elbow-room, and could not endure to be shut up in polite drawing-rooms and dining-rooms, where the guests jostled each other, mentally and bodily, and where all true individuality was hidden and wasted, the frivolities of conventional society could not be otherwise than a burden and an irritant. Under such conditions he became contradictory and pugnacious, most of all when he detected any signs of hypocrisy, foppishness, or dilettantism. The sharp sayings, and still more "accusing silences," as Emerson terms them, which Thoreau dealt out to all pretentious personages, had, of course, the effect of getting him the reputation of cynicism and misanthropy; those readers, however, who rightly appreciate his character, will distinguish between a normal churlishness, which certainly was not one of his failings, and an occasional acridity of speech, as, for instance, when he informed a too insistent acquaintance that he had "no time for friendships."

To style Thoreau a misanthrope is to misunderstand his whole nature. He loved to study all forms of innocent and healthy character, and in one of his works he quotes, as specially applicable to himself, Terence's famous maxim of regard for our common humanity. Had he been the mere fastidious recluse that some critics have supposed him, he could not have drawn his sympathetic and humorous sketches of the sturdy Concord farmers, or of the hearty unsophisticated wood-chopper by whom he was visited at Walden, or of the aged brown-coated fisherman who haunted the banks of the Musketaquid, or of the drunken Dutchman on board a New York steamboat, or of the merry old oysterman who gave him hospitality at Cape Cod. For idealist though he was, he possessed a true vein of humour, which is none the less piquant because it is expressed in a manner so dry, pithy, and laconic. It is pleasant, too, to note that the gravity which was habitual with the hermit and philosopher could melt, when occasion arose, into merriment and good-fellowship, and that when he laughed "the operation was sufficient to split a pitcher." He was fond of playing on his flute, and would at times sing "Tom Bowling"* and other nautical songs with much gusto and animation; and it is recorded that on several occasions he startled his friends by performing an improvised dance.[5]

Reference has already been made to his sympathy with children, and his remarkable power of interesting and amusing them. He would tell them stories, sing to them, and play on his flute, or perform various pieces of jugglery for their entertainment—an accomplishment which he had probably learnt from his eccentric uncle, Charles Dunbar, in whose oddities he always took much interest. But it was in the huckleberry expeditions that his services were in greatest request, for then he would drive the hay-cart in which the children journeyed to the hills where the berries abounded,—and who knew each knoll and dingle so intimately as Thoreau?—"leading the frolic with his jokes and laughter as they jolted along." When we read the delightful accounts of his kindness and helpfulness on these occasions, we know how to treat the charges of misanthropy and churlishness.

"Though shy of general society," says Moncure Conway,

> Thoreau was a hero among children, and the captain of their excursions. He was the *sine qua non* of the Concord huckleberry party, which is in that region something of an institution. To have Thoreau along with them was to be sure of finding acres of bushes laden with the delicious fruit. . . . A child stumbles and falls, losing his carefully gathered store of berries; Thoreau kneels beside the weeping unfortunate, and explains to him and to the group that nature has made these little provisions for next year's crop. If there were no obstacles, and little boys did not fall occasionally, how would berries be scattered and planted? and what would become of huckleberryings? He will then arrange that he who has thus suffered for the general good shall have the first chance at the next pasture.

*The name of this song is usually given as "Tom Bowline."—Eds.

The severity of Thoreau's ideal was not less conspicuous in matters of business than in his relations towards his friends. He was austerely faithful to his inner sense of right, keeping his engagements with stern regularity, and never failing in the full discharge of his duty to those who engaged him as surveyor or handicraftsman. Himself thus inflexible in his probity, he expected and exacted a corresponding uprightness in others; and where this was not exhibited, he made no polite pretence of concealing his dissatisfaction. No meanness, hypocrisy, or dishonesty, whether on the part of rich or poor, could escape the rigorous censure of "that terrible Thoreau," as his acquaintances called him; nor would he waste on thriftless applicants one cent of the money which he had earned by his own conscientious labours. He maintained sincerity to be the chief of all virtues.

"A Yankee stoic" is a term that has been applied to Thoreau. Though cosmopolitan in his philosophical views, he was American to the backbone in sentiment and manner, and did not study to conceal his indifference or aversion for European fashions. He possessed in large measure the American qualities of self-consciousness and self-assertion, and avows in *Walden* his intention "to brag as lustily as chanticleer in the morning," in order to wake up his neighbours. And as America was the most favoured of countries, so did he extol his native Concord as the most favoured of towns. This preference, however, was not due, as some have supposed, to mere parochialism and narrowness of mind—for parochialism, the study of the little instead of the great, was certainly not one of Thoreau's failings—but was, as Emerson has pointed out, a half-serious, half-humorous way of reasserting the old stoical maxim that all places are the same to a wise man, and that "the best place for each is where he stands." On the same principle, being asked at table what dish he preferred, he is said to have answered, "The nearest."

Not even the suspicion of provincial prejudice can attach to Thoreau's literary tastes. It is true that his earnest practical mind could not relish the subtleties of metaphysical works, the dullness of moral treatises, or the floweriness of romance; and he was usually averse to reading the magazines and journals of the day, the "news" in which he was interested being other than that which newspapers report. But he read largely and widely nevertheless, and his discrimination never deteriorated into fastidiousness and partiality. The class of books which he most highly valued was undoubtedly the "sacred scriptures," as he calls them, of the poets and philosophers of Persia and India—the Bhagvat

Geeta, Vishnu Sarma, Laws of Menu, Saadi, and other "bibles" of the old Oriental religions. These he studied chiefly in French and German translations, which he accumulated with such zeal that he is said to have had the best library of such books in the country. There are numerous citations from these ancient writings in Thoreau's own works, and so great was his reverence for them that he jealously asserted their claim to the title of "scriptures" in common with those of Jewish origin. When a young visitor from Harvard College informed him that he was studying "the Scriptures," Thoreau quickly retorted, "But *which?*"

Thoreau's classical studies were not confined to his early years, but were fully maintained in after-life, Homer, Æschylus, Virgil, and the poets of the Greek Anthology being his chief favourites. Classical learning is eulogised in both the *Week* and *Walden,* as being the most heroic and tranquillising of all branches of reading. "The value of the classic languages," says Wentworth Higginson, "was never better exemplified than in their influence on his training. They were real 'humanities' to him, linking him with the great memories of the race, and with high intellectual standards, so that he could never, like some of his imitators, treat literary art as a thing unmanly and trivial. I remember how that fine old classical scholar, the late John Glen King, of Salem, used to delight in Thoreau as being 'the only man who thoroughly loved both nature and Greek.'" His reading in Greek and Latin included not only the "classics" proper, but many old-fashioned authorities on agriculture and natural history, such as Aristotle, Ælian, Theophrastus, Cato, Varro and Pliny.

His respect for Linnæus was, according to Channing, "transcendent." He loved to study Froissart and the old-fashioned chronicles, and such voyages as those of Drake and Purchas, with any books of travel that came in his way. Among poets the old English writers were most to his liking; he read and appreciated old ballad-writers, Chaucer, Spenser, Ossian, Herbert, Cowley, Quarles, and, above all others, Milton, whose "Lycidas" was often on his lips. For the moderns he cared comparatively little, the chief exceptions being Goethe, Wordsworth, Coleridge, Ruskin, and Carlyle. He admired Ruskin, but thought him somewhat bigoted, finding in him, as he expressed it, "too much about art for me and the Hottentots."

There was another and wholly different branch of reading to which Thoreau devoted a considerable portion of his time—the records of the native Indian tribes, which he extracted with much labour and research from the histories of the Jesuit missionaries, the early New England chroniclers, and various other sources of information. Everything connected with the Indians had a strange interest and fascination for him; he noted and admired their natural instinct of woodcraft, their immobility and self-possession, and their mysterious sense of remoteness from the white man; he several times visited Maine in order to study their language and habits, and never failed to converse with the wandering parties who sometimes pitched their tents for a few weeks on the banks of the Concord river. His collection of Indian relics had been commenced while he was still a youth, for the soil of Concord—an old settlement of Indian tribes—was rich in these treasures, arrow-heads, pottery, and stone implements being often turned up by the plough. Regularly every spring, when the fields had been washed bare by rains and thawing snow, would Thoreau set out to gather his crop of arrowheads, and his extraordinary keenness of sight in detecting these relics was often a cause of wonder to less observant minds. "I do not see where you find your Indian arrow-heads," once remarked the companion of his walk. "Here is one," replied Thoreau on the instant, picking one up and presenting it to his astonished friend.[6]

This remarkable sympathy, on the part of one of the most advanced of modern thinkers, with the spirit of a savage and decaying race is accounted for by Thoreau's strong natural inclination to the uncultivated and wild. He loved the sea and all desert places; preferred the wild apple to the cultured orchard, and the dreariest swamp to the most fragrant garden; and it cheered him to see the young forest-pines springing up anew in the fertile corn-land. The Indian, the human representative of wild life in New England, thus attracted his sympathies, just as the sympathies of George Borrow were attracted to the roaming gipsy tribes.

This inclination of Thoreau to wild nature was not, as some critics have suggested, a symptom of an unhealthy temperament, but rather a method of retaining the excellent soundness of his mind. "His whole life," says Lowell, "was a search for the doctor." This was not the case. He went to nature, not as a sickly valetudinarian, seeking a cure for his ailments, but as a sane and healthy man, the secret of whose health lay in this very familiarity with the open air. "Nothing was more delightful," so Channing wrote, "than the enormous curiosity, the continued greenness, the effervescing wonder of this child of Nature." Walking was a necessity of Thoreau's existence; he demanded four hours at least each day for sauntering at leisure over hills and woods and fields, taking short cuts when he could, and avoiding for the most part the grit and noise of the busier high-roads. The old Marlboro' road which led south-west from Concord, through a spacious tract of open country abounding in patches of scrub-oak and wild apples, was one of his favourite haunts; so, too, were Walden woods and the "Cliffs" which overhang Fairhaven, the wide bay formed by a bend of the river two miles south of the village. The river was much frequented by him at all seasons of the year; for in summer he made almost daily voyages in his boat, which he kept moored in Ellery Channing's riverside garden, and in winter the frozen stream offered a convenient pathway.

On these expeditions Thoreau was generally unaccompanied, unless Ellery Channing or one of his few chosen friends happened to be with him. Offers of companionship were not rarely forthcoming, but these he for the most part declined with that frankness which was all his own. "Would he not walk with them?" some acquaintances would ask. "He did not know; there was nothing so important to him as his walk; he had no walks to throw away on company." But for those who succeeded in gaining this privilege a rare treat was assured. Here is a reminiscence of Thoreau from a private letter of G. W. Curtis:—

> It always seems to me one of the good fortunes of my life that I knew Concord when Emerson, Hawthorne, and Thoreau were citizens there, and that I personally knew them. If in personal intercourse Thoreau sometimes seemed to be, as Hawthorne said, "a cast-iron man," he was after all no more rigid than the oak which holds fast by its own roots whatever betides. One of my most vivid recollections of my life in Concord is that of an evening upon the shallow river with Thoreau in his boat. We lighted a huge fire of fat pine in an iron crate beyond the bow of the boat and drifted slowly through an illuminated circle of the ever-changing aspect of the river bed. In that house beautiful you can fancy what an interpreter he was.

"His powers of conversation," says another who was thus favoured, "were extraordinary. I remember being surprised and delighted at every step with revelations of laws and significant attributes in common things. . . . The acuteness of his senses was marvellous; no hound could scent better, and he could hear the most faint and distant sound without even laying his ear to the ground like an Indian. As we penetrated farther and farther into the woods he seemed to gain a certain transformation, and his face shone with a light that I had not seen in the village." The account of Thoreau's skilful and genial leadership of the Concord huckleberry-parties has already been quoted, and from the same authority we have an equally charming description of how he would guide his friends to the haunts of the water-lily.[7]

> Upon such occasions his resources for our entertainment were inexhaustible. He would tell stories of the Indians who once dwelt thereabouts, till the children almost looked to see a red man skulking with his arrow on shore; and every plant or flower on the bank or in the water, and every fish, turtle, frog, lizard about us, was transformed by the wand of his knowledge from the low form into which the spell of our ignorance had reduced it, into a mystic beauty. One of his surprises was to thrust his hand softly into the water, and as softly raise up before our astonished eyes a large bright fish, which lay as contentedly in his hand as if they were old acquaintances.

This fish was probably the Bream, whose nest-guarding habits are described by Thoreau in *The Week.* "The Breams are so careful of their charge that you may stand close by in the water and examine them at your leisure. I have stood over them half-an-hour at a time, and stroked them familiarly without frightening them, . . . and have even taken them gently out of the water with my hand."

His extraordinary sympathy with animals was one of the most singular and pleasing features in Thoreau's character. Like St. Francis, he felt a sense of love and brotherhood towards the lower races, and regarded them not as "brute beasts," without sensibility or soul, but as possessing "the character and importance of another order of men." He protested against the conceited self-assurance with which man sets down the intelligence of animals as mere "instinct," while overlooking their real wisdom and fitness of behaviour. They were his "townsmen and fellow-creatures," whose individuality must be recognised as much as his own, and who must be treated with courtesy and gentleness.

The strange influence which Thoreau was able to exercise over beasts, and birds, and fishes was doubtless chiefly due to the power of his humane sympathy, partly, also, to his habits of patient silence and watchfulness, in which he resembled the hermits of the Middle Ages.

His hut at Walden was inhabited by other creatures besides himself; the birds would flit fearlessly through the room; the red squirrel raced over the roof, while moles and hares stabled in the cellar; and chickadees perched on the armfuls of wood which he carried across his threshold. Once, as he was hoeing in a garden, a sparrow alighted on his shoulder, which he regarded as "a greater honour than any epaulet he could have worn." Nor was this all, for his mingled firmness and sympathy enabled him to take all sorts of liberties with the wildest of wild creatures. A story is told how a squirrel, which he had taken home for a few days in order to observe its habits, refused to be set at liberty, returning again and again to its new friend with embarrassing persistence, climbing up his knee, sitting on his hand, and at last gaining the day by hiding its head in the folds of his waistcoat—an appeal which Thoreau was not able to withstand.

Thoreau was essentially a "poet-naturalist," as Ellery Channing entitled him, and not a man of science. He was, indeed, an honorary member and correspondent of the Boston Natural History Society; but he declined, as a rule, to write memoirs of his experiences in this branch of study, on the ground that he could not properly detach the mere external record of observation from the inner associations with which such facts were connected in his mind—in a word, the natural history of the subject could not be separated from the poetry.[8] His whole method, as we have seen, was different from that of the scientific anatomist; he observed but he did not kill, making it his object to hold his bird "in the affections" rather than in the hand. It is said that when some Concord loafers mockingly asked Thoreau if he really did not shoot a bird when he wanted to study it, he replied, "Do you think I should shoot *you* if I wanted to study you?"

His diaries testify to the immense diligence and keenness of his communion with nature, and his unflagging interest in the seasons and all they bring with them. He noted and recorded the habits of animals, the tracks of the fox and otter, the migrations and song of birds, the croak of frogs and chirp of crickets, the spawning and nests of fishes, the blossoming of flowers, the fall of leaves, the height of the river, the temperature of ponds and springs, and innumerable other phenomena of outdoor life. Like all true naturalists, he loved birds, and many are the entries in his journal respecting the kinds that are native at Concord—the bobolink, the robin, the song-sparrow, the whip-poor-will, the cat-bird, and the blue-bird, which, as he beautifully said of it, "carries the sky on its back." He loved to be awakened in the early summer mornings by the song of birds, and nothing cheered him so much in the midst of a winter storm as a bird's chirp or whistle.

The neighbourhood of Concord, with its wide tracts of meadow and woodland, was a fine field for the naturalist; and Thoreau, in his characteristic love of paradox, was fond of asserting that it surpassed all other places as a centre of observation—a foible for which he was gently bantered by Emerson. He talked about nature, it was wittily remarked, "as if she had been born and brought up at Concord." *Ne quid quœsiveris extra te Concordiamque* was his humorous maxim. He contended that all the important plants of America were included in the flora of Massachusetts, and after reading Kane's *Arctic Voyage* he expressed his conviction that most of the Arctic phenomena might be noted at Concord—an assertion which he partly substantiated by the discovery of red snow and one or two Labrador plants. He had thoughts of constructing a complete calendar for the natural phenomena of Concord, and believed that if he waked up from a trance the time of year would be as plain to him from the plants as the time of day from a dial. Of all flowers the water-lily was his favourite, but there were none that he did not know and love; even the growth of the sturdy aboriginal weeds gave him a sense of satisfaction. He often walked miles to note the condition of some rare tree or shrub, and congratulated himself that the time thus spent was more profitably laid out than in a good many social visits. The friend who first met him after he had found the rare "climbing fern" used to tell what a glow was on his face as he pulled off his hat to show the trophy, which was coiled round his head like a chaplet.

Such were the points in Thoreau's personality which made him an object of interest and wonder from the first to his own friends and acquaintances,[9] and afterwards to a far wider circle. We can well believe that a man gifted with such an intense and genuine individuality often found himself, as Emerson tells us, in "dramatic situations," and that in any debatable matter there was no person whose judgment was awaited by his townsmen with keener expectation. As his fame spread he gained an increasing number of admiring friends, some of whom travelled long distances to see and converse with him, in the belief that "this was the man they were in search of, the man of men, who could tell them all they should do."

NOTES

1. See appendix: "Portraits of Thoreau."

2. Daniel Ricketson wrote of him:—"He was fond of hardy enterprises, and few of his companions could compete with him. In fact I have heard that he quite tired out an Indian guide, on one of his excursions to Maine." *Daniel Ricketson and His Friends,* p. 14.

3. From "Memorials of the Class of 1837, Prepared for the Fiftieth Anniversary of the Graduation," by Henry Williams, Boston, 1887.

4. Emerson, according to one statement; according to another, Miss Elizabeth Hoar.

5. See, for instance, the account given in the *Outlook,* Dec. 2, 1899, by a friend of Sophia Thoreau's, who describes how one evening, in his father's house, Henry began to dance until, "growing more and more inspirited, he finally sprang over the center table, alighting like a feather on the other side."

6. See the fine passage on arrow-heads in the *Journal,* March 28, 1859. "They are not fossil bones, but, as it were, fossil thoughts, forever reminding me of the mind that shaped them."

7. Moncure Conway, *Fraser,* April 1866.

8. See his own remarks on his relations with scientific societies, *Journal,* March 5, 1853.

9. Some amusing stories are recorded of the bewilderment caused to simple minds by Thoreau's books and sayings. Here is a sample of conversation: " 'Mr. Thoreau, you say in one of your books that you once lost a horse and a hound and a dove. Now I should like to know what you mean by that.' " " 'Why, everybody has met with losses, has he not?' " " 'A pretty answer to give a fellow!' "

6

Life at Concord

In the autumn of 1847, shortly after leaving the hut at Walden, Thoreau again took up his residence at Emerson's house, and lived there a year during his friend's absence in Europe, in order to keep Mrs. Emerson company and take charge of the garden. He was in the habit of assisting Mr. Alcott in garden work on his estate at "Hillside," and in 1847 the two friends and fellow-workers had built Emerson a summer-house, to be used as a study. Early in October Thoreau accompanied Emerson to Boston to see him start on his voyage, and in a letter to his sister Sophia he feelingly described the appearance and dimensions of the philosopher's cabin, and how, instead of a walk in Walden woods, he would be compelled to promenade on deck, "where the few trees, you know, are stripped of their bark." Emerson, on his part, was not forgetful of Thoreau during his visit to England, and we find him planning, in 1848, a new joint American and English magazine, to which Thoreau was to be one of the chief contributors. After Emerson's return to Concord in 1849* Thoreau lived at his father's house in the village, and this continued to be his home for the rest of his life.[1]

He had now begun to consider literature his regular occupation, and it was as a writer and lecturer that he was henceforth chiefly known. We have seen that during his literary novitiate he had contributed articles (unpaid, for the most part) to the *Dial* and other journals; and in 1847, by the kind services of Horace Greeley, his appreciative essay on Carlyle

*Emerson returned from Europe in late July 1848.—Eds.

was printed in *Graham's Magazine.* It was in reference to this essay that Carlyle wrote to Emerson on May 18, 1847: "You must tell Mr. Thoreau that his Philadelphia magazine, with the lecture in two pieces, was faithfully delivered here about a fortnight ago, and carefully read, as beseemed, with due entertainment and recognition. A vigorous Mr. Thoreau—who has formed himself a good deal upon one Emerson, but does not want abundant fire and stamina of his own. . . . In plain prose, I like Mr. Thoreau very well, and hope yet to hear good and better news of him." This was followed in 1849 by the essay on "Civil Disobedience," an expression of his anarchist views, which found place in the *Boston Æsthetic Papers.*

In the spring of the same year he took a more daring and important step by the publication of his first volume, the *Week on the Concord and Merrimac{k} Rivers,* which was issued, at the author's expense, by Munroe, a Boston bookseller. The book was well reviewed, but did not sell, and the result was that Thoreau was compelled to raise money to pay off the debt by devoting his time for an unusually long period to the more remunerative but less congenial task of surveying. An edition of one thousand copies had been printed, and for several years the bulk of these lay idle on the publisher's shelves, until, in 1853, the remaining seven hundred volumes were returned *en masse* to the author. This event was recorded by Thoreau in his characteristic vein of dry humour, and with a manly courage and self-reliance not to be surpassed in the history of literary authorship.

> The wares are sent to me at last, and I have an opportunity to examine my purchase. They are something more substantial than fame, as my back knows, which has borne them up two flights of stairs to a place similar to that to which they trace their origin. Of the remaining two hundred ninety and odd, seventy-five were given away, the rest sold. I have now a library of nearly nine hundred volumes, over seven hundred of which I wrote myself. Is it not well that the author should behold the fruits of his labour? My works are piled up in my chamber, half as high as my head, my *opera omnia.* This is authorship. These are the work of my brain. There was just one piece of good luck in the venture. The unbound were tied up by the printer four years ago in stout paper wrappers, and inscribed "H. D. Thoreau's Concord River, fifty copies." So Munroe had only to cross out 'River' and write

"Mass.," and deliver them to the express-man at once. I can see now what I write for, and the result of my labours. Nevertheless, in spite of this result, sitting beside the inert mass of my works, I take up my pen to-night, to record what thought or experience I may have had, with as much satisfaction as ever. Indeed, I believe that this result is more inspiring and better than if a thousand had bought my wares. It affects my privacy less, and leaves me freer.[2]

That *The Week* should at first have failed to win the favour of any but a few sympathetic readers can hardly be a matter of surprise, since its intense idealism and strongly pantheistic tone were ill calculated to conciliate the ordinary American mind. Purporting to be a record of the trip made by the two brothers in 1839, it was in reality an outpouring of its author's ideal philosophy on a great variety of topics, a number of essays and poems (mostly reprints from the *Dial*) being interwoven, in the most arbitrary manner, with the thread of the nominal subject. The book is thus rendered vague, disjointed, and discursive; and is, moreover, almost arrogant in its transcendental egoism. Yet, with all its deficiencies, it has, and must ever have, a great and indefinable charm for the lovers of Thoreau's genius. Its very lack of cohesion and entire disregard of method contribute to enhance the effect of its poetical mysticism and brilliant descriptive power, while several of the discourses introduced into it—notably those on Friendship and Religion—are written in Thoreau's most admirable and telling style.[3]

In the autumn of 1849 Thoreau accompanied a friend on an excursion to the wild sandy tract of Cape Cod, for which he conceived so great a liking that he visited it again on several occasions; in like manner he spent a week in Canada, with Ellery Channing as his fellow-traveller, in September 1850. Each of these excursions provided material for a series of articles in *Putnam's Magazine;* but both came to an abrupt conclusion owing to misunderstandings between author and publisher—a mishap to which Thoreau's outspoken tone and uncompromising temper made him peculiarly liable. His visit to the Maine Woods in 1846 was described in the *Union Magazine* two years later; and he again went to Maine in 1853 and 1857. These occasional excursions were a great pleasure to Thoreau, as extending the circle of his observations, without putting any restriction on his freedom; but he still resolutely declined to extend his travels to more distant regions, in spite of the offers he sometimes received from admirers and friends, who wished to take him round the world at their own cost. Believing that "the far-fetched is of least value," he asserted that the sight of a marsh-hawk in the Concord meadows was of more interest to him than the entry of the allies into Paris. It is easy to laugh at this deliberate concentration of thought on a particular locality; but a study of Thoreau's life inclines one to believe that he gauged correctly the peculiar strength and the peculiar weakness of his shy and sensitive genius.

The course of his life at Concord was singularly quiet and uneventful. Always an affectionate son and brother, he lived contentedly as a member of the household. "No one could more heartily enjoy his family life than Henry," writes one who knew him. "He invariably came down from his study for a while in the evening for conversation; the sound of the piano was sure to draw him."[4] Thoreau's study was in the garret, where he stored his collections of birds' eggs, botanical specimens, and Indian relics, and carried on his literary work. His regard for his father was in nowise diminished by the dissimilarity of their characters, a contrast which is illustrated by some suggestive passages in the journal. On one occasion we find a protest made by the quiet, unobtrusive, but eminently practical old man against what he considered a waste of time on the part of his more imaginative son, who was busying himself in making sugar from a neighbouring maple-grove when he could have bought it cheaper at the village shop. To his father's remark that it took him from his studies, Thoreau made the characteristic answer that it *was* his study, and that after being engaged in this pursuit he felt "as if he had been to a university." Mrs. Thoreau, who was of the same age as her husband, retained all her dramatic vivacity of manner, love of society, and extraordinary power of talk. It is said that when his mother began to talk at table, Thoreau would patiently remain silent until she had finished, and then, with a courteous obeisance, resume the thread of his conversation at the point where it had been interrupted. On June 14th, 1849, the family circle suffered a heavy loss in the death of Helen, Thoreau's elder sister, whose character, like that of the brother who died seven years earlier, was full of ability and promise.

It was about this time that Thoreau became acquainted with Mr. Harrison G. O. Blake, a clergyman and tutor residing at Worcester, Massachusetts, with whom he corresponded largely from 1848 onwards, chiefly on subjects connected with his ideal method of thought, and who was fitted by his gentle nature, and subtle yet receptive intellect, to be Thoreau's most devoted disciple. In a letter dated Nov. 25,

1889, Mr. Blake kindly furnished the following reminiscences of their friendly intercourse:—

I was introduced to him first by Mr. Emerson more than forty years ago, though I had known him by sight before at college. I recall nothing of that first interview unless it be some remarks upon astronomy, and his want of interest in the study as compared with studies relating more directly to this world—remarks such as he has made here and there in his writings. My first real introduction was from the reading of an article of his in the *Dial* on "Aulus Persius Flaccus," which dated March 27, 1848, appears now in the *Week.* That led to my first writing to him, and to his reply, which is published in the volume of letters. Our correspondence continued for more than twelve years, and we visited each other at times, he coming here to Worcester, commonly to read something in public, or being on his way to read somewhere else.

As to the outward incidents of our intercourse, I think of little or nothing that it seems worth while to write. Our conversation, or rather his talking, when we were together, was in the strain of his letters and of his books. Our relation, as I look back on it, seems almost an impersonal one, and illustrates well his remark that "our thoughts are the epochs in our lives; all else is but as a journal of the winds that blew while we were here." His personal appearance did not interest me particularly, except as the associate of his spirit, though I felt no discord between them. When together, we had little inclination to talk of personal matters. His aim was directed so steadily and earnestly towards what is essential in our experience, that beyond all others of whom I have known, he made but a single impression on me. Geniality, versatility, personal familiarity are, of course, agreeable in those about us, and seem necessary in human intercourse, but I did not miss them in Thoreau, who was, while living, and is still in my recollection and in what he has left to us, such an effectual witness to what is highest and most precious in life. As I re-read his letters from time to time, which I never tire of doing, I am apt to find new significance in them, am still warned and instructed by them, with more force occasionally than ever before; so that in a sense they are still in the mail, have not altogether reached me yet, and will not probably before I die. They may well be regarded as addressed to those who can read them best.

In addition to his pedestrian excursions, Thoreau paid occasional visits to Cambridge and Boston, the attraction at the former place being the University Library, from which, owing to the insistence with which he petitioned the librarian and president, he was permitted unusual privileges in the taking out of books. At Boston he was fond of studying the books of the Natural History Society and walking on the Long Wharf; the rest "was barrels." Salem, too, he sometimes visited as the guest of Hawthorne, who had left Concord in 1846, and he lectured once or twice at the Salem Lyceum, of which Hawthorne was the secretary. One other journey he had about this time of a more mournful character. In July 1850, when Margaret Fuller, who had become the wife of the Marquis of Ossoli, was shipwrecked on her return from Italy and drowned off the coast of Fire Island, near New York, Thoreau with her other friends hurried to the scene of the disaster, to assist in the vain attempt to recover her body.[5]

"Here I am, thirty-four years old," he wrote in his Journal (July 19, 1851), "and yet my life is almost wholly unexpanded. How much is in the germ! Life is not long enough for one success. Within another thirty-four years that miracle can hardly take place." Though he had now attained a certain recognised position as a writer, he was still compelled to earn the greater part of his means of subsistence by land-surveying. This employment—or rather the company into which his employment brought him—was very far from being a congenial one; on such occasions he was no longer the poet and idealist, but merely "Thoreau the surveyor," as he informs his friend Blake. Lecturing was a more congenial occupation, though here, too, he speaks of himself as "simply their hired man"; while his candour occasionally placed him in strained relations towards his audience. Though he several times made his mark on the platform, the more usual result was to puzzle and bewilder those who heard him. "I have offered myself much more earnestly as a lecturer than as a surveyor," he remarks in his Journal, Dec. 18, 1853. "Yet I do not get any employment as a lecturer; was not invited to lecture once last winter, and only once (without pay) this winter. But I can get surveying enough, which a hundred others in this county can do as well as I." That there were some, however, who could enter into the spirit of his lectures, we know from Dr. Emerson's appreciative reference to "Thoreau's gift to his townspeople in the old Lyceum, on those dreary winter nights when he read us his 'Wild Apples' or 'Autumnal Tints.'" He gave, in all, nearly twenty addresses in Concord, and was for some years the chief organiser of the lectures at the Lyceum.

We have a glimpse of Thoreau in the autumn of 1852 from Arthur Hugh Clough, who had come over to Boston with Thackeray and thence paid Emerson a visit at Concord. "Walk with Emerson to a wood with a prettyish pool," writes Clough in his diary for 14th November, the pool being presumably Walden. "Concord is very bare; it is a small sort of village, almost entirely of wood houses, painted white, with Venetian blinds, green outside, with two white wooden churches. There are some American elms and sycamores, *i.e.* planes; but the wood is mostly pine—white pine and yellow pine—somewhat scrubby, occupying the tops of the low banks and marshy hayland between. A little brook runs through to the Concord river. At 6:30, tea and Mr. Thoreau; and presently, Mr. Ellery Channing, Miss Channing, and others." It was in this same year that Nathaniel Hawthorne returned to Concord, and took up his residence at "Hillside"—now renamed "Wayside"—an estate which had been for some years in Alcott's possession, and on which Thoreau and Alcott had done a great deal of manual work in constructing terraces and summer-houses.

Thoreau's sympathies were enlisted from his earliest manhood in the cause of abolition, and he was himself instrumental more than once in furthering the escape of fugitive slaves. An instance of this kind has been recorded by Mr. Conway, who was introduced to Thoreau by Emerson in the summer of 1853.

> When I went to the house next morning I found them all in a state of excitement by reason of the arrival of a fugitive negro from the South, who had come fainting to their door about daybreak, and thrown himself on their mercy. . . . I sat and watched the singularly lowly and tender devotion of the scholar to the slave. He must be fed, his swollen feet bathed, and he must think of nothing but rest. Again and again this coolest and calmest of men drew near to the trembling negro, and bade him feel at home, and have no fear that any power should again wrong him. He could not walk this day, but must mount guard over the fugitive, for

slave-hunters were not extinct in those days, and so I went away after a while, much impressed by many little traits that I had seen as they appeared in this emergency, and not much disposed to cavil at their source, whether Bible or Bhaghavat.

At this time Thoreau's mind was a good deal occupied with the question of slavery, for in 1850 the iniquitous Fugitive Slave Law had been passed by Act of Congress, and in the spring of 1854 the heart of Massachusetts had been stirred by the case of Anthony Burns, an escaped slave, who was sent back by the authorities of the State in compliance with the demand of his owner. This event formed the main topic of Thoreau's essay on "Slavery in Massachusetts," which was delivered as an address at the anti-slavery celebration at Framingham in 1854, on which occasion the Constitution of the United States was publicly burned by Lloyd Garrison, an incident which may explain the passionate tone of Thoreau's paper. "For my part," he said, "my oldest and worthiest pursuits have lost I cannot say how much of their attraction, and I feel that my investment in life here is worth many per cent less since Massachusetts last deliberately sent back an innocent man, Anthony Burns, to slavery." In his kindred essay on "Civil Disobedience," when dealing with this same subject of state-supported slavery, he had expressed the conviction that if but *one* honest man in the State of Massachusetts were to withdraw his allegiance as a protest against this iniquity, and to be imprisoned therefor, "it would be the abolition of slavery in America." This was written before the appearance of John Brown.

On August 9, 1854, occurred the most memorable event of Thoreau's literary life—the publication of *Walden* by Messrs. Ticknor & Co.* of Boston. The greater part of the book was drawn from the journal kept by him during his residence in the woods, but there are also passages which were written at a later date, when he was working his materials into their ultimate form. The inducement to give the story of his sojourn at Walden to the world was, he tells us, that very particular inquiries had been made by his townsmen concerning the manner of his life, and that he felt he had something to say which bore not remotely on the social condition of the inhabitants of Concord. The result justified the expectations of the author in writing the book, and

*Ticknor & Fields.—Eds.

of the publishers in printing it, for in spite of the ridicule and hostility of some critics, a great deal of interest was aroused by *Walden,* and the edition appears to have been sold out in the course of a few years, in marked contrast to the unsaleableness of its predecessor, *The Week.* From whatever point of view it be regarded, *Walden* is undoubtedly Thoreau's masterpiece; it contains the essence of his ideal philosophy; it is written in his most powerful and incisive style, and by the freshness and *naïveté* of its narrative it excites the sympathy and imagination of the reader.

"Welcome, Englishmen! welcome, Englishmen!" Thoreau exclaimed in *Walden,* "for I had had communication with that race." "A young Englishman, Mr. Cholmondeley, is just now waiting for me to take a walk with him," he writes in a letter dated 1st October 1854. This was Mr. Thomas Cholmondeley, of Overleigh, Cheshire, a nephew of Bishop Heber, and six years Thoreau's junior in age, the only Englishman, it appears, with whom he ever became intimate. He spent some time with Thoreau at Concord, and the strong personal admiration which this travelled English gentleman conceived for the Concord "hermit" is one of many testimonies to Thoreau's impressive character. A correspondence was maintained after Mr. Cholmondeley's return to Europe in 1855, and towards the end of that year Thoreau received a splendid gift of books on oriental subjects, in English, French, Latin, Greek and Sanscrit, from his English friend, who knew how deep an interest he felt in Buddhist literature. Mr. Cholmondeley again visited Concord in 1859.[6]

Increasing fame brought Thoreau an increasing number of friends, while his intimacy with Emerson, Alcott, and Channing continued as close as ever. One of these later friends and correspondents was Mr. Daniel Ricketson, of New Bedford, a genial lover of good books and of literary friendships. Their first meeting was at Christmas 1854, when Thoreau, then on his way to lecture at Nantucket, paid a passing visit to New Bedford, and spent a day or two at "Brooklawn," Mr. Ricketson's house. On presenting himself to his host, he was at first mistaken, as on several other occasions, for "a pedlar of small wares," but this unfavourable impression was quickly corrected when he gave proof of his singular conversational powers. The points in his personal appearance which particularly arrested Mr. Ricketson's attention were his keen blue eyes, "full of the greatest humanity and intelligence," and, next to these, his sloping shoulders (in which he resembled Emerson), long arms, and short sturdy legs, which generally enabled him to outwalk his companions in his daily excursions.[7]

In Mr. Frank B. Sanborn, who as a young man came to live at Concord early in 1855, Thoreau found another friend with whom he gradually became intimate. The first impressions of Thoreau, as recorded at the time by one who was destined to be his biographer a quarter of a century later, are extremely interesting. "Thoreau looks eminently *sagacious,* like a sort of wise wild beast. He dresses plainly, wears a beard in his throat, and has a brown complexion." The fringe of beard here referred to, which is seen in the Worcester portrait of Thoreau, taken in 1856, was grown as a protection for his throat. In the earlier crayon of 1854 he appears as beardless.[8]

His friendship with Horace Greeley, editor of the *New York Tribune,* had been kept up since his visit to Staten Island chiefly by letter, for Thoreau was seldom at New York; but Greeley had done him valuable service at a critical period in obtaining publication for several of his articles in *Graham, Putnam,* and other magazines, and in acting generally as a literary friend and adviser. Greeley had a farm at Chappaqua, thirty-six miles north of New York, and in the early part of 1856 he pressed Thoreau to come to reside at this place and act as tutor to his children, which offer seems to have been for a time seriously entertained.

It was in the following November, when Thoreau accompanied Alcott on a short visit to Chappaqua, that he had a memorable interview with as powerful and remarkable a personality as his own. The meeting of Thoreau with Walt Whitman, of the author of *Walden* with the author of *Leaves of Grass,* is told by Thoreau in his letters and by Alcott in his diary.* It is remarkable, when one considers the strong dissimilarity between the two men—types as they are of different sides of human nature, the thrifty, simple, self-complete type, as opposed to the largely inclusive and sympathetic—that Thoreau should have so rightly appreciated, after one short conversation, the breadth of Whitman's genius, and should have recognised in him "the greatest democrat the world has seen," one who suggested "something a little more than human."

"To be sure," wrote Thoreau,

*This meeting of Alcott and Thoreau with Whitman took place at the latter's home on Myrtle Avenue in the Brooklyn suburbs.—Eds.

I sometimes feel a little imposed on. By his heartiness and broad generalities he puts me into a liberal frame of mind, prepared to see wonders—as it were, sets me upon a hill or in the midst of a plain—stirs me well up, and then—throws in a thousand of brick. Though rude and sometimes ineffectual, it is a great primitive poem, an alarum or trumpet-note ringing through the American camp. Wonderfully like the Orientals, too, considering that when I asked him if he had read them, he answered, "No; tell me about them."

I did not get far in conversation with him—two more being present—and among the few things I chanced to say, I remember that one was, in answer to him as representing America, that I did not think much of America, or of politics, and so on, which may have been somewhat of a damper to him.

Since I have seen him I find that I am not disturbed by any brag or egoism in his book. He may turn out the least of a braggart of all, having a better right to be confident. He is a great fellow.[9]

In the following year Thoreau had the satisfaction of meeting another of the great figures of American democracy. John Brown, then fresh from his anti-slavery struggle in Kansas, was a guest at Mr. Sanborn's house in March 1857, and was introduced by his host to Emerson, Alcott, Thoreau, and other Concord friends. It was arranged that Brown should address a meeting in the Town Hall on the subject of slave-holding. "On the day appointed," says Mr. Sanborn,[10] "Brown went up from Boston at noon, and dined with Mr. Thoreau, then a member of his father's family, and residing not far from the railroad station. The two idealists, both of them in revolt against the civil government because of its base subservience to slavery, found themselves friends from the beginning of their acquaintance. They sat after dinner discussing the events of the border warfare in Kansas, and Brown's share in them, when, as it often happened, Mr. Emerson called at Mr. Thoreau's door on some errand to his friend. Thus the three men met under the same roof, and found that they held the same opinion of what was uppermost in the mind of Brown." Emerson and Thoreau were both present at the meeting in the evening, when Brown produced a thrilling effect on his audience by his earnestness and eloquence, and by the display of the very chain worn by one of his sons who had been made prisoner and tortured by the champions of slavery. From that time there were many people in Concord who were favourable to Brown's cause.

On the occasion of a visit to Mr. Ricketson at New Bedford in 1857, Thoreau, moved by the air of "The Campbells Are Coming," surprised the company by an unexpected outburst of hilarity, under which impulse he sang "Tom Bowling,"* and finally entered upon an improvised dance, "keeping time to the music carefully but executing some steps more like Indian dances than the usual ballroom figures." He afterwards told his sister Sophia that in the excitement of this dance he had made a point of treading on the toes of the guileless Alcott, who was sitting on the sofa.

Here is an extract from Alcott's diary at the time:—

> *1st April 1857.*—At Mr. Ricketson's, two and a half miles from New Bedford, a neat country residence, surrounded by wild pastures and low woods; the little stream Achushnet flowing east of the house and into Fair Haven Bay at the City. Ricketson's tastes are pastoral, simple even to wildness, and he passes a good part of his day in the fields and woods, or in his rude shanty near his house, where he writes and reads his favourite authors, Cowper having the first place in his affections. He is in easy circumstances, and has the manners of an English gentleman—frank, hospitable, and with positive persuasions of his own; a man to feel on good terms with, and reliable as to the things good and true—mercurial, perhaps, and wayward a little sometimes.
>
> *3rd April, A.M.*—In house and shanty. Thoreau and Ricketson treating of nature and the wild. Thoreau has visited Ricketson before, and won him as a disciple, though not in the absolute way he has Blake of Worcester, whose love for his genius partakes of the exceeding tenderness of woman, and is a pure Platonism to the fineness and delicacy of the devotee's sensibility. But Ricketson is himself, and plays the manly part in the matter, defending himself against the master's tough "thoroughcraft" with spirit and ability.

Mr. Blake's estimate of Thoreau's character has already been quoted; equally interesting is that given by Mr. Ricketson, with which this chapter may fitly conclude.

*The name of this song is usually given as "Tom Bowline."—Eds.

On this point I can bear my own testimony, that without any formality he was remarkable in his uprightness and honesty; industrious and frugal; simple though not fastidious in his tastes, whether in food, dress, or address; an admirable conversationist, and a good story-teller, not wanting in humour. His full blue eye, aquiline nose, and peculiarly pursed lips added much to the effect of his descriptive powers. He was a man of rare courage, physically and intellectually. In the way of the former, he arrested two young fellows on the lonely road leading to his hermitage by Walden Pond, who were endeavouring to entrap a young woman on her way home, and took them to the village. Intellectually his was a strong manly mind, enriched by a classical education, and extensive knowledge of history, ancient and modern, and English literature—himself a good versifier, if not true poet, whose poetic character is often seen in his prose works.[11]

NOTES

1. This was the "Yellow House," in Main Street, which was enlarged from a cottage by Thoreau and his father.

2. These unused copies of the *Week* were bought by a Boston publisher, shortly after Thoreau's death, and issued as a second edition in 1862. But by oversight a tell-tale page of advertisement was bound up with them, announcing the early publication of *Walden,* which had in fact been issued by the same firm in 1854! Here is a curious fact in bibliography—that every copy of the so-called second edition of the *Week* is an *editio princeps.*

3. By far the most noteworthy of contemporary appreciations of *The Week* is the letter addressed to Thoreau by J. A. Froude, Sept. 3, 1849, and first printed in *Some Unpublished Letters of Henry and Sophia Thoreau,* 1899. "When I think of what you *are*—of what you have *done* as well as what you have *written,*" said Froude, "I have the right to tell you that there is no man living upon this earth at present, whose friendship or whose notice I value more than yours."

4. *The Outlook,* Dec. 2, 1899.

5. See his account of the wreck in a letter addressed to Emerson from Fire Island Beach, July 25, 1850.

6. In later years he took the name of Owen. He succeeded to the Condover estate, near Shrewsbury, in 1863, and died in the following year.

7. See *Daniel Ricketson and His Friends,* 1902, where there is a reproduction of an entertaining pencil sketch, by Daniel Ricketson, of "H. D. Thoreau, as he presented himself at the door of Brooklawn, Dec. 25th, 1854."

8. See Appendix: "Portraits of Thoreau."

9. We can only regret that Whitman, on his part, left no written record of his impressions of Thoreau; but it is interesting, in this connection, to note his mention of him in his *Specimen Days.* See also Horace Traubel's *With Walt Whitman in Camden,* where there are reminiscences of Whitman's estimate of Thoreau, favorable and unfavorable, as gleaned from his conversation in later years, and *The Life of Anne Gilchrist,* p. 237. It would seem that there was more true insight in Thoreau's reading of Whitman than in Whitman's of Thoreau.

10. *Memoirs of John Brown,* 1878.

11. See *Daniel Ricketson and His Friends,* pp. 252, 253.

7

Excursions

To avoid the need of too frequently breaking the story of Thoreau's Concord life, it is convenient to group together some of the chief excursions made by him between 1846 and 1860. And first as to his mode of journeying. The perfection of travelling, he thought, was to travel without luggage; and after considerable experience he decided that "the best bag for the foot-traveller is made with a handkerchief, or, if he study appearances, a piece of stiff brown paper well tied up." He would travel as a common man, and not as a gentleman, for he had no wish to spend a moment more than was necessary in the railway-carriage, among the sedentary travellers, "whose legs hang dangling the while," or to be a prey to the civility and rapacity of the landlords of hotels; he preferred to journey on foot, and to spend the night in the homes of farmers and fishermen, where he could sit by the kitchen fire, and hear the sort of conversation in which he was always interested. "The cheapest way to travel," he wrote in *The Week,* "and the way to travel the farthest in the shortest distance, is to go afoot, carrying a dipper, a spoon, and a fish-line, some Indian meal, some salt, and some sugar. When you come to a brook or pond, you can catch fish and cook them; or you can boil a hasty-pudding; or you can buy a loaf of bread at a farmer's house for four-pence, moisten it in the next brook that crosses the road, and dip it into your sugar—this alone will last you a whole day." He wore a shabby grey coat and a drab hat, and carried with him a piece of tallow for greasing his boots, for he no more thought of blacking these than his face; and "many an officious shoe-black," he tells us, who carried off his shoes while he was slumbering, mistaking him for a gentleman, "had occasion to repent it before he produced a gloss on them." He was better pleased when the farmers called out to him, as he passed their fields, to come and help in the hay-making; or when he was mistaken for a travelling mechanic, and asked to do tinkering jobs, and repair clocks or umbrellas; or when, as once happened, a man wished to buy the tin cup which he carried strapped to his belt.

His pack was quickly made up, for he kept a list of the few necessaries that he carried, among which were sewing materials, a book for pressing plants, spy-glass, compass, and measuring-tape. He had learnt the art of camping out in his earlier excursions, and was well skilled in pitching a tent or constructing a hut at the shortest possible notice. On these occasions his favourite drink was tea, which he made strong and sweet in his tin cup, so that, as Channing hints, the traveller was not only refreshed but "grew intimate with tea-leaves." He was fond of carrying with him a large slice of cake, with plums in it, for he found that this furnished him with dinner and dessert at the same time. Thus simply equipped, he was practically independent of time-tables and hotel-lists, could roam wherever the fancy took him, and take his own time in his observation of the fauna and flora of the districts which he visited. Such expeditions were not only an agreeable change in themselves, but were a means of adding to his various collections and suggesting new subjects for his pen; so that it was natural that the pleasant experience which he gained in his week's jaunt in 1839 should have been repeated more frequently in later years.

Cape Cod, the long sandy spit which was visited by Thoreau in 1849, 1850, and 1855, is described by him as "the bared and bended arm of Massachusetts, behind which the State stands on her guard, with her back to the Green Mountains, and her feet planted on the floor of the ocean, like an athlete protecting her Bay." All wild and desolate landscapes had an attraction for him, and he delighted in the dreary expanse of this long monotonous tract of shore, with its drift-wood and kelp-weed, flocks of gulls and plovers, and incessant din of waves. His accounts of these vast sandy tracts are extremely vivid and picturesque; the very dash and roar of the waves seem to be reproduced, as though we were reading, as the author suggests, "with a large conch-shell at our ear."

It was amidst these surroundings that Thoreau, after witnessing the pathetic scenes that followed the wreck of an Irish brig at Cohasset, walked and meditated with a companion (Ellery Channing, presumably, though the name is not recorded) in the wet, windy days of a stormy October. "Day by day," it has been said, "with his stout pedestrian shoes, he plodded along that level beach—the eternal ocean on one side, and human existence reduced to its simplest elements on the other—and he pitilessly weighing each." They journeyed northward, on the Atlantic side of the Cape, till they came to Provincetown at its upper extremity, avoiding towns and villages on their route, and spending the nights in the cottages of fishermen and lighthouse-keepers, where Thoreau was several times mistaken for a travelling pedlar. "Well," said an old fisherman, unconvinced by the explanations that had been offered, "it makes no odds what it is you carry, so long as you carry truth along with you." At Wellfleet, where the wayfarers were entertained in the hut of an aged oysterman, an idiot son of their host expressed his determination to get a gun and shoot the "damned book-pedlars, all the time talking about books." What might have been a more serious misunderstanding was caused by a robbery of the Provincetown Bank about the time of their visit to Cape Cod, for Thoreau learnt afterwards that the suspicion of the police had centred on him and his companion, and that their journey had been traced the whole length of the Cape.

The volume on *Cape Cod,* parts of which appeared in *Putnam's Magazine* in 1855, and in the *Atlantic Monthly* in 1864, is deliberately formless in style, being interspersed with quotations from old histories and records of merely local interest; it abounds, however, in its author's dry sententious humour and sparkling paradoxes. It has been said that *Cape Cod* is in one sense the most human of Thoreau's books, and has more tenderness of tone than *Walden,* as if the sea had exercised a mellowing influence on his mind. Especially good are the Dutch pictures of the Wellfleet oysterman and the "sea-captains" of Provincetown. "It is worth the while," says Thoreau, "to talk with one whom his neighbours address as Captain, though his craft may have long been sunk, and he may be holding by his teeth to the shattered mast of a pipe alone, and only gets half-seas-over in a figurative sense now. He is pretty sure to vindicate his right to the title at last—can tell one or two good stories at least." In *Cape Cod* the experiences of several visits are condensed into one account.

On 25th September 1850, Thoreau and Ellery Channing started on a week's tour in Canada, equipped each of them in the simple fashion which Thoreau adopted on his excursions (he avows that he wore his "bad weather clothes" on this occasion), and styling themselves, accordingly, the "Knights of the Umbrella and the Bundle." They first visited Montreal, where the Church of Notre Dame made a great impression on Thoreau's imagination, as described by him in a very characteristic passage—

> It was a great cave in the midst of a city,—and what were the altars and the tinsel but the sparkling stalactites?—into which you entered in a moment, and where the still atmosphere and the sombre light disposed to serious and profitable thought. Such a cave at hand, which you can enter any day, is worth a thousand of our churches which are open only Sundays, hardly long enough for an airing, and then filled with a bustling congregation—a church where the priest is the least part, where you do your own preaching, where the universe preaches to you and can be heard. In Concord, to be sure, we do not need such. Our forests are such a church, far grander and more sacred. I think of its value not only to religion, but to philosophy and to poetry; besides a reading-room, to have a thinking-room in every city! Perchance the time will come when every house even will have not only its sleeping-rooms, and dining-room, and talking-room or parlour, but its thinking-room also, and the architects will put it in their plans. Let it be furnished and ornamented with whatever conduces to serious and creative thought. I should not object to the holy water, or any other simple symbol, if it were consecrated by the imagination of the worshippers.[1]

From Montreal they went on to Quebec, and thence to the Falls of St. Anne, thirty miles lower down the St. Lawrence. In the latter district they obtained lodging in a house where their French host and his family could speak but a few words of English, and they concluded that "a less crime would be committed on the whole if they spoke French with him, and in no respect aided or abetted his attempts to speak English," a resolve which they carried into effect with some amusing difficulties—for in spite of his Gallic extraction, a knowledge of the French tongue was not one of Thoreau's accomplishments—solving their frequent misunderstandings by writing on the table with a piece of chalk. What chiefly impressed Thoreau, during his brief visit to Canada, was the contrast between the imperialism of the Canadian cities, whose inhabitants appeared to him "to be suffering between two fires—the soldiery and the priesthood," and the more homely free-thinking independence of American life.

The *Excursion to Canada,* in which his experiences and impressions are related, was partly published in *Putnam* in 1853. It is certainly one of the least successful of its author's writings; for though it contains a few fine passages and interesting touches, it is overladen with description, the cities being, as Horace Greeley expressed it, "described to death." "I fear that I have not got much to say about Canada," says Thoreau, in his opening sentence, "not having seen much; what I got by going to Canada was a cold."

The object of Thoreau's three excursions to the Maine Woods, the wild district which lies at the extreme north-east of New England, was chiefly to gratify his strong curiosity and interest in the habits and character of the Indians. In September 1846, during his fortnight's absence from the Walden hermitage, he visited Maine and in company with a cousin, who was employed in the Bangor lumber trade, made a voyage up the western branch of the Penobscot river, and ascended Ktaadn, one of the loftiest mountains of New England, over 5000 feet in height. The paper on "Ktaadn and the Maine Woods," which appeared in the *Union Magazine* in 1848, is a record of this expedition, and contains some vivid descriptions of the outlying lumber-farms and log-huts; the manufacture and management of the *batteau,* or "bark-canoe," by which they navigated the rapids of the Penobscot; their trout-fishing extraordinary in the clear swift streams which descend from the heights of Ktaadn; and, above all, the primitive solitudes of the Maine forests, which were still the haunt of the bear, the moose, the deer, the wolf, and other wild animals.

> Perhaps I most fully realised that this was primeval, untamed, and for ever untamable *Nature,* or whatever else men call it, while coming down this part of the mountain. We were passing over 'Burnt Lands,' burnt by lightning, perchance, though they showed no recent marks of fire, hardly so much as a charred stump, but looked rather like a natural pasture for the moose and deer, exceedingly wild and desolate, with occasional strips of timber crossing them, and low poplars springing up, and patches of blueberries here and there. I found myself traversing them familiarly, like some pasture run to waste, or partially reclaimed by

> man; but when I reflected what man, what brother or sister or kinsman of our race made it and claimed it, I expected the proprietor to rise up and dispute my passage. It is difficult to conceive of a region uninhabited by man. We habitually presume his presence and influence everywhere. And yet we have not seen pure Nature, unless we have seen her thus vast and drear and inhuman, though in the midst of cities. . . .
>
> What is most striking in the Maine wilderness is the continuousness of the forest, with fewer open intervals or glades than you had imagined. Except the few burnt-lands, the narrow intervals on the rivers, the bare tops of the high mountains, and the lakes and streams, the forest is uninterrupted. It is even more grim and wild than you had anticipated, a damp and intricate wilderness, in the spring everywhere wet and miry. . . . Who shall describe the inexpressible tenderness and immortal life of the grim forest, where nature, though it be mid-winter, is ever in her spring, where the moss-grown and decaying trees are not old, but seem to enjoy a perpetual youth; and blissful, innocent nature, like a serene infant, is too happy to make a noise, except by a few tinkling, lisping birds and trickling rills?

In the autumn of 1853 Thoreau, accompanied by the same relative, and by an Indian hunter named Joe Aitteon, paid his second visit to the Maine Woods, the lake of Chesuncook being this time his destination.* The paper entitled "Chesuncook," which was published in the *Atlantic Monthly* in 1858, is occupied in great measure with the subject of moose-hunting, and contains, among other things, some characteristic reflections on the "murder of the moose," in which Thoreau had been a witness and to some extent a participator.

"The Allegash and East Branch," the account of his third and final excursion to Maine, in July 1857, at which time he had been in weak health for two years, forms the concluding portion of the volume afterwards published under the title of *The Maine Woods,* and is chiefly concerned with geographical topics, botanical specimens, and the character of Joe Polis, an intelligent Indian guide, from whom Thoreau derived much valuable information. "As to Thoreau's courage and man-

*Thoreau left Boston for their trip to Maine on September 13; he returned to Concord on September 27. See Harding, *The Days of Henry Thoreau,* 309–12.—Eds.

liness," says Mr. Edward Hoar, of Concord, who was his fellow-traveller on this expedition, "nobody who had seen him among the Penobscot rocks and rapids, the Indian trusting his life and his canoe to his skill, promptitude, and nerve, would ever doubt it."

Very characteristic of Thoreau was his fondness for mountains and the occasional excursions which he made to the ranges visible from the Concord hills, and to the remoter and still loftier White Mountains, formed some of the most pleasant episodes in his life. He possessed in a marked degree the instinct of locality, and with map and compass would make out his way unerringly through the wildest regions, and could run up the steepest places without losing breath. "He ascended such hills as Monadnock or Saddleback mountains," says Channing, "by his own path, and would lay down his map on the summit and draw a line to the point he proposed to visit below, perhaps forty miles away in the landscape, and set off bravely to make the short cut. The lowland people wondered to see him scaling the heights as if he had lost his way, or at his jumping over their cow-yard fences, asking if he had fallen from the clouds."

In July 1858 he made an expedition with his friend Edward Hoar to the White Mountains of New Hampshire, the Switzerland of New England, which he had visited with his brother nineteen years earlier. They travelled by carriage, and Thoreau complains in his journal of the loss of independence, as regards choice of camping-stations, which this method involved; it was not simple and adventurous enough to suit his tastes. He also disliked the "mountain houses" which were already erected in New Hampshire, with large saloons, and other appurtenances of the city, for the supposed convenience of the tourist; "give me," he says, "a spruce-house made in the rain." Their chief exploit during the fortnight they spent in New Hampshire was the ascent of Mount Washington, the highest mountain in New England, where, in descending towards Tuckerman's Ravine, Thoreau lost his footing on the steep crust of a snow-slope, and was only saved by digging his finger-nails into the snow. They camped for several days in a plantation of dwarf firs near the foot of the ravine, and by the carelessness of their guide in lighting a fire several acres of brushwood were burnt. The next afternoon Thoreau sprained his ankle while scrambling on the rocks, and was laid up in the camp for two or three days.

Few men have written of mountains more worthily than Thoreau has done. "I suppose," he says, "that I feel the same awe when on their summits that many do on entering a church. If you have been to the top of Mount Washington, let me ask, what did you find there? Going up there and being blown upon is nothing. We never do much climbing while we are there, but we eat our luncheon &c, very much as at home. It is after we get home that we really go over the mountain, if ever. What did the mountain say? What did the mountain do?"

Monadnock, a mountain of nearly four thousand feet, which is visible from Concord on the north-west horizon, had been visited by Thoreau, like Wachusett, in his early manhood. In 1858, a month before his excursion to the White Mountains, he camped a couple of nights on its summit in company with Mr. Blake, and two years later he again ascended it with Ellery Channing, who, being unaccustomed to mountain life, did not relish its inconveniences as much as his friend, but complains pathetically of the fatigue, "the blazing sun, the face getting broiled; the pint-cup never scoured; shaving unutterable; your stockings dreary, having taken to peat," and other similar discomforts. This visit to Monadnock was the last excursion of Thoreau's in which he camped out. The reasons which compelled the discontinuance of a practice in which he found such pleasure will appear when we resume the story of his life at Concord.

NOTE

1. *Putnam's Magazine,* 1853.

8

Closing Years

As early as 1855 Thoreau's health had begun to be a matter of some anxiety to himself and to his friends. Frequent mention has been made by those who knew him personally of the iron endurance and sturdy strength of limb which enabled him to outstrip the companions of his walks and open-air pursuits. Emerson, who was himself little qualified for an outdoor life, marvelled at his friend's indefatigable energy in tree-felling and field-work; while Channing and others who accompanied him to the mountains suffered acutely from the exposure which Thoreau seemed not to feel. Nevertheless, this power of prolonged endurance was due far more to an indomitable spirit than to a natural strength of constitution; for, idealist as he was, he was too apt to compel his body at all times to keep pace with his mind, and if he was somewhat exacting in his demands on his friends, he had still less consideration for his own weaknesses. "The physique given him at birth," says Dr. E. W. Emerson, "was unusually slight. I have never seen a person with more sloping shoulders, and seldom a narrower chest. Yet he made his frame all that it could be made." It is on record that his college career was interrupted by an illness which kept him for some time from his studies; and as early as 1841 there is reference in the journal to a bronchial attack, which is significant when read in connection with the story of his closing years.

In the autumn of 1855 we find him writing of the "months of feebleness" that had preceded, and of his satisfaction at partly regaining his health, though he would have liked "to know first what it was that ailed him." During the winter that followed he was able to walk afield as usual, and boasts that he had made it a part of his business "to wade in the snow and take the measure of the ice," and that, in spite of his recent ill-health, he was probably the greatest walker in Concord. In the spring of 1857 he refers to his "two-year-old invalidity," from which we see that the disquieting symptoms had not wholly abated; and it cannot be doubted that he at all times subjected himself to considerable risks both by the severity of his exertions in carrying heavy loads and taking long walks, and also in the recklessness with which he exposed himself to all extremes of weather, and all changes of season, regardless alike of frost and sun, wind and snow, the chills of midnight and the mists of the early morning. For the present, however, we hear no more of his illness, and he continued to lead the same equable contented life which has already been described.

After the appearance of *Walden* in 1854, Thoreau did not publish any further volume, though he was busily engaged in various literary plans, chief among which was his projected book on the Indians. His relations with editors and publishers, partly no doubt owing to his own unaccommodating temper, had not always been of the most amicable kind; his essays were repeatedly refused by papers and magazines on account of their unorthodox tone, and it is said that an editor once begged Emerson to persuade Thoreau to write an article containing no allusion to God. In 1858, when, at Emerson's suggestion, he contributed his paper on "Chesuncook" (the Maine Woods) to the *Atlantic Monthly,* of which Mr. Lowell was then editor, a fresh point of difference arose. A sentence in which Thoreau had spoken in his idealistic style of the "living spirit" of the pine tree ("it is as immortal as I am, and perchance will go to as high a heaven, there to tower above me still") was struck out under editorial censorship, without the permission of the author, and this being an indignity to which Thoreau would never submit, he sent no more of his essays to the *Atlantic Monthly* until the editorship had passed into other hands. The sentence in question was of course restored when the article on "Chesuncook" was included in the volume on *The Maine Woods.*

It is said that as Thoreau's character matured and hardened, his relations with Emerson grew somewhat "Roman" and austere. That at a certain period there was some estrangement between them may be seen from passages in Thoreau's journal, where he deplores the loss of their friendship. "And now another friendship is ended," he writes. "I do not know what has made my friend doubt me, but I know that in love there is no mistake, and that every estrangement is well founded. . . . With one with whom we have walked on high ground we cannot deal on any lower ground ever after."[1] The matter is perhaps best summed up in the words of Dr. E. W. Emerson: "Although their personal relations could not be close, each held the other in highest honor."

On 3rd February 1859 Thoreau records in his diary the death of his father, who had lived to the age of seventy-two. This was the third time he had mourned the loss of a near relative, his brother having died, as narrated, in 1842, and his sister Helen in 1849. In the following letter to Mr. Daniel Ricketson he gives an interesting account of his father's character:—

Concord, *12th February 1859.*

Friend Ricketson,—I thank you for your kind letter. I sent you the notice of my father's death as much because you knew him as because you know me. I can hardly realise that he is dead. He had been sick about two years, and at last declined rather rapidly though steadily. Till within a week or ten days before he died he was hoping to see another spring, but he then discovered that this was a vain expectation, and thinking that he was dying, he took his leave of us several times within a week before his departure. Once or twice he expressed a slight impatience at the delay. He was quite conscious to the last, and his death was so easy that though we had all been sitting around the bed for an hour or more expecting that event, as we had sat before, he was gone at last almost before we were aware of it.

I am glad to read what you say about his social nature. I think I may say that he was wholly unpretending, and there was this peculiarity in his aim, that though he had pecuniary difficulties to contend with the greater part of his life, he always studied merely how to make a *good* article, pencil or other (for he practised various arts), and was never satisfied with what he had produced. Nor was he ever in the least disposed to put off a *poor* one for the sake of pecuniary gain, as if he laboured for a higher end.

Though he was not very old, and was not a native of Concord, I think that he was, on the whole, more identified with Concord street than any man now alive, having come here when he was about twelve years old, and set up for himself as a merchant here at the age of twenty-one, fifty years ago.

As I sat in a circle the other evening with my mother and sister, my mother's two sisters, and my father's two sisters, it occurred to me that my father, though seventy-one, belonged to the youngest four of the eight who recently composed our family.

How swiftly at last, but unnoticed, a generation passes away! Three years ago I was called, with my father, to be a witness to the signing of our neighbour Mr. Frost's will. Mr. Samuel Hoar, who was there writing it, also signed it. I was lately required to go to Cambridge to testify to the genuineness of the will, being the only one of the four who could be there, and now I am the only one alive.

My mother and sister thank you heartily for your sympathy. The latter in particular agrees with you in thinking that it is communion with still living and healthy nature alone which can restore to sane and cheerful views. I thank you for your invitation to New Bedford, but I feel somewhat confined here for the present. I did not know but we should see you the day after Alger was here. It is not too late for a winter walk in Concord. It does me good to hear of spring birds and singing ones too, for spring seems far away from Concord yet. I'm going to Worcester to read a parlour lecture on the 22nd, and shall see Blake and Brown. What if you were to meet me there? or go with me from here? You would see them to good advantage. Cholmondeley has been here again, after going as far south as Virginia, and left for Canada about three weeks ago. He is a good soul, and I am afraid that I did not sufficiently recognise him.

Please remember me to Mrs. Ricketson, and to the rest of your family.—Yours, Henry David Thoreau.

After his father's death Thoreau carried on the family business, pencil-making and the preparation of plumbago, on behalf of his mother and his younger sister Sophia. This same year, 1859, was destined to be one of the most memorable in his experience. We have seen how he was, from the first, an ardent abolitionist, how he had withdrawn his allegiance from the State of Massachusetts owing to its sanction of slavery, and had delivered lectures and published essays on the subject at a time when the profession of abolitionist principles was neither safe nor comfortable; and how he had himself assisted escaped slaves in their flight to Canada. True-hearted American though he was, he had little respect for the patriotic feelings of those of his fellow-countrymen who could combine a pride in their national liberties with an indifference to negro slavery; and on one of the occasions when a runaway was surrendered to his owners by the Massachusetts Government, he is said to have proposed to his townsmen at Concord that the monument which commemorated American independence should be coated with black paint.

When he was introduced to John Brown in 1857 he doubtless recognised in him the "one righteous man" whose advent he had heralded in the essay on *Slavery in Massachusetts,* which he had written and published several years before, and it is not difficult to imagine the admiration with which he followed the great emancipator's career. Himself an individualist, and, as regards politics, less a man of action than a man of thought, he reverenced in Brown the very qualities in which he was himself deficient. The final effort of Brown's heroism was now at hand, and the events that followed proved to be in some respects the crowning point of Thoreau's life also. As Channing said, "Thoreau ranks in the front of the storming-party against the old Golgotha of slavery. He never faltered, but from first to last lived and worked a faithful friend to the American slave."

In October 1859 John Brown, who was just entering on his sixtieth year, was again in Concord,* and it was from Mr. Sanborn's house that he started on his last and fateful expedition against the Virginian slaveholders. On 16th October Brown was arrested at Harper's Ferry, and then ensued those seven weeks of suspense and anxiety and vituperation which ended in his trial and death. To Thoreau—the anchorite and idealist—belongs the lasting honour of having spoken the first public utterance on behalf of John Brown, at a time when a torrent of ridicule and abuse was being poured by the American press on the so-called crazy enthusiast whose life was to pay forfeit for his boldness. Notice was given by Thoreau that he would speak in the Town Hall on Sunday

*John Brown was in Concord in May 1859, but Salt is probably in error about his being there again in October. Brown spent most of the last few months before the Harper's Ferry raid on October 16, 1859, holed up with his followers in a farmhouse about seven miles from Harper's Ferry on the Maryland side of the Potomac.—Eds.

evening, 30th October, on the subject of John Brown's condition and character; and when this course was deprecated by certain republicans and abolitionists as hasty and ill-advised, they received the emphatic assurance that he had not sent to them for advice, but to announce his intention of speaking. A large and attentive audience, composed of men of all parties, assembled to hear Thoreau's address,—the "Plea for Captain John Brown," which is in every respect one of the very finest of his writings. In the plainest and most unequivocal terms, and with all his accustomed incisiveness of style and expression, he avowed his absolute approval of the conduct of a man who was indicted as a rebel and traitor. When we read the magnificent and heart-stirring passages in which he eulogised the heroic character of John Brown, we can well believe Emerson's statement that the address was heard "by all respectfully, by many with a sympathy that surprised themselves."

On November 1st Thoreau gave the same address at Boston. "This exciting theme," says the *Liberator* of November 4th, "seemed to have awakened 'the hermit of Concord' from his usual state of philosophic indifference, and he spoke with real enthusiasm for an hour and a half. A very large audience listened to this lecture, crowding the hall half-an-hour before the time of its commencement, and giving hearty applause to some of the most energetic expressions of the speaker." The lecture was also given at Worcester, and again at Boston, in the course of the same week.*

The time was short, and from the first it could scarcely have been hoped that Brown's life would be spared. Those few weeks were probably the only period in Thoreau's career when he turned in vain to nature for the customary comfort and repose; and he has put on record the stunned, incredulous feelings with which he received, on 2nd December, the news of the execution. On that day a solemn service in commemoration of Brown's martyrdom was held in the Town Hall at Concord, when addresses were delivered by Thoreau, Alcott, Emerson, and other abolitionists, and a funeral hymn, composed by Sanborn, was sung by those assembled. It was on this occasion that Thoreau quoted Marvell's lines, so applicable to his own action:—

*According to Walter Harding, Thoreau gave "A Plea for Captain John Brown" only once, not twice, in Boston. Thoreau delivered the address at Tremont Temple on November 1. See *The Days of Henry Thoreau,* 419.—Eds.

When the sword glitters o'er the judge's head,
And fear has coward churchmen silenced,
Then is the poet's time; 'tis then he draws,
And single fights forsaken virtue's cause.

Thoreau regarded the whole episode of Brown's capture and trial as a touchstone designed to bring out into a strong light the nature of the American Government. That it afforded a touchstone of his own character few will deny. It has been well remarked by John Burroughs that "this instant and unequivocal indorsement of Brown by Thoreau, in the face of the most overwhelming public opinion even among anti-slavery men, throws a flood of light upon him. It is the most significant act of his life. It clinches him. It makes the colours fast." The "Plea for Captain John Brown," which bears in every sentence unmistakable signs of the intensity of feeling under which it was written, must have convinced even those of Thoreau's hearers who were least in accord with him that they saw before them no cynical misanthrope who had placed himself in unreasonable antagonism to the social opinions of his townsmen, but a man of humaner sympathies and larger aspirations than their own.

And indeed the judgment of the good people of Concord had already changed concerning the eccentric recluse who some twelve years before had excited their contemptuous surprise by his sojourn in the Walden woods; they had learnt to appreciate the kindness and courtesy that underlay his rough exterior, and the wisdom which found expression in his trenchant and out-spoken words. He thus came to be respected and honoured in the very quarter where honour is proverbially most difficult to attain for the prophet who is not willing to prophesy smooth things; and his fellow-citizens recognised the superiority of character "which addressed all men with a native authority."

Nor had the lapse of years and the increase of experience failed to exercise a mellowing effect on Thoreau's own temperament; and his intimate friends have noted how the foibles and crudeness which marked the less pleasing side in his self-assertive personality were gradually losing their sharpness as he grew older, while he still retained all the freshness and originality of his genius, and looked forward to the future with the same unbounded confidence as ever. This prospect, unhappily, was not destined to be realised; but there is satisfaction in the thought that it was his championship of John Brown which formed the last public act of Thoreau's career.

It was on December 3rd 1860 that his fatal illness had its beginning. He took a severe cold while counting the rings on trees, at a time when the ground was covered with a deep snow; this led to a bronchial affection, which was increased by his persistence in keeping a lecturing engagement at Waterbury, and the precautions which he afterwards exercised were too late, as consumption which was inherent in his family, had then set in. In the spring of 1861 he was advised by his doctor to travel, and he was now willing to do in sickness what he had always refused to do in health, though even now he preferred to remain within the boundaries of the States.

Mr. Blake being unable to accompany him in this journey to Minnesota, his place was taken by Horace Mann, a connection of Nathaniel Hawthorne's. In a letter addressed to Mr. Sanborn from Minnesota, on 26th June, Thoreau speaks of himself as better in health than when he left home, but still far from well, having performed the journey in a very dead-and-alive manner, though he much enjoyed the weeks they spent in the neighbourhood of St. Paul's and the novel sights of the Mississippi. From St. Paul's Thoreau and his companion made a further expedition some three hundred miles up the Minnesota or St. Peter's River, in order to witness a gathering of the Sioux Indians at Redwood, where an annual payment was made to the tribe by the United States Government. One of the sights which most interested him, during this tour in the West, was that of the aboriginal crab-apple, as told by him in the essay on "Wild Apples," which appeared in the *Atlantic Monthly* in 1862.

Meantime the spark which had been kindled by John Brown's heroism had not been quenched by his death, and the war between the northern and southern States had already commenced in the spring of 1861. The misfortunes of the North in the first months of the war affected Thoreau so powerfully that he used to say he could never recover while the war lasted, and he told his friends in these dark days that he was "sick for his country." There is not the least justification for Lowell's statement that Thoreau "looked with utter contempt on the august drama of destiny, of which his country was the scene, and on which the curtain had already risen." "Was it Thoreau or Lowell," asks Wentworth Higginson, "who found a voice when the curtain fell, after the first act of that drama, upon the scaffold of John Brown? Had Thoreau retained health and life, there is no telling but what the civil war might have brought out a wholly new aspect of him, as it did for so many."

The journey to Minnesota was not productive of any lasting improvement in his health. When he visited Mr. Ricketson at New Bedford in August, 1861, his racking cough impressed his friend with the conviction that his strength was fast failing, though his face, "except for a shade of sadness in the eyes," (noticeable in the portrait which was taken at this time by Mr. Ricketson's request),[2] did not betray the change. But in the course of the winter that followed it became evident that the disease had reached a point at which it could not be arrested, and that there was no longer any hope of saving his life. "It was my good fortune to see him again last November," wrote G. W. Curtis (*Harper's Magazine,* July 1862), "when he came into the library of a friend to borrow a volume of Pliny's Letters. He was much wasted, and his doom was clear. But he talked in the old strain of wise gravity without either sentiment or sadness." Then it was that the exaltation of spirit over matter, of the mind over the body, which had throughout his life been one of Thoreau's prominent characteristics, was still more strongly manifested as he neared his death; whatever his friends might feel, he himself appeared to be unaffected by his illness; he looked at himself, as it were, from an outer standpoint, surveying, without alarm and without anxiety, this intrusion into his bodily system of a weakness to which his mind at least should never be subject.

It was one of Thoreau's maxims that work of some kind is as necessary for those who are sick as for those who are strong, and it is recorded by his sister Sophia, who, with their mother's help, tenderly nursed him in his illness, that to the last day of his life he never ceased to call for the manuscripts on which he was engaged. He was about to become a contributor to the *Atlantic Monthly* magazine, which was now edited by Mr. Fields in the place of Mr. Lowell, and during the last few months of his life he accomplished, in his sister's words, "a vast amount of labour," in preparing these papers for the press, and in completing the records of his visits to the Maine Woods. There was something fitting in the fact that in this closing scene of his life his thoughts should be occupied with the Indian, whom he resembled not only in his sympathy with wild nature, but also in his stoical reserve, unfaltering self-command, and passive acquiescence in whatever his destiny had in store for him.

His unfailing patience and fortitude are described as wonderful by those who witnessed them; it was impossible to be sad in his presence, or to realise that one so cheerful and contented was on the verge of death. When he could not sleep he would ask his sister to arrange the furniture so as to cast weird shadows on the walls, and he expressed the wish that his bed were in spiral form, that he might curl up in it as in a shell; at other times, when rest was not altogether denied him, he would interest his friends by a narration of his strange and fantastic dreams, saying that "sleep seemed to hang round his bed in festoons." As long as sufficient strength remained to him, he resolutely took his seat at table with his mother and sister, insisting that "it would not be social to take his meals alone," and when he could no longer walk, his bed was brought down into the front parlour of the house, where he was visited by many of his neighbours and townsmen, from whom, during the whole course of his illness, he received such touching and gratifying tokens of kindness and affection that he would sometimes protest he would be ashamed to stay in the world after so much had been done for him. "I never saw a man dying with so much pleasure and peace," was the remark made afterwards by one of his visitors; which recalls to mind the last words of Thoreau's last letter: "I am enjoying existence as much as ever, and regret nothing."

Several of his utterances on these occasions were very characteristic. When Channing, the faithful and intimate companion of his walks and studies, hinted at the weary change that had now come over his life, and how "solitude began to peer out curiously from the dells and wood-roads," he whispered in reply, "It is better some things should end." He said to Alcott that he "should leave the world without a regret." Nor in these last weary months of suffering did he lose his shrewd humour and native incisiveness of speech. "Well, Mr. Thoreau, we must all go," said a well-meaning visitor, who thought to comfort the dying man by the ordinary platitudes. "When I was a boy," answered Thoreau, "I learnt that I must die, so I am not disappointed now; death is as near to you as it is to me." When asked whether he "had made his peace with God," he replied that "he had never quarrelled with him." He was invited by another acquaintance[3] to enter into a religious conversation concerning the next world. "One world at a time," was the quiet retort.

It would, however, be an injustice to Thoreau to represent his death-bed as nothing but a scene of stoical fortitude and iron self-restraint—there were other and not less admirable traits of tenderness and love.

From his window, which looked out on the village street, he saw passing and repassing some of his favourite children, whom he had so often conducted in their merry expeditions after the huckleberry or water-lily. "Why don't they come to see me?" he said to his sister. "I love them as if they were my own;" and it is pleasant to read that they often visited him, and enjoyed these last meetings scarcely less than the first. The sound of music had the same charm for him to the end, and on hearing a street musician play some old tune that had been familiar to him in childhood, he is said to have shed tears and asked his mother to give the man some money.

The thought of death was never a cause of anxiety to him; but terrible indeed to a man of Thoreau's temperament must have been the death-in-life of that long and dreary winter, when the daily walk and converse with nature, which had seemed necessities of his existence, were but memories of the past, and even the carefully kept journal must needs be discontinued, since there was in fact nothing to record. Yet of this outer life, in which for twenty-five years he had so faithfully and unremittingly busied himself, he now spoke no word, and we are told that no stranger could have imagined from his manner that "he ever had a friend in field or wood." Once only, as he stood at his window, did he allude to what must have been so constantly in his thoughts. "I cannot see on the outside at all," he said to his friend Channing. "We thought ourselves great philosophers in those wet days, when we used to go out and sit down by the wall-sides." There is on this point a singular and pathetic similarity between Thoreau's last illness and that of Richard Jefferies, who of all men was nearest to him in passionate devotion to open-air life; but Thoreau's sterner and more reticent nature would not give his thoughts the expression in which Jefferies found relief.

It was on 6th May 1862, a beautiful spring morning, that the end came. At eight o'clock, shortly after enjoying the odour of a bunch of hyacinths from a friend's garden, he asked to be raised upright in his bed; his breathing became gradually fainter and fainter, until he died without pain or struggle in the presence of his mother and sister, his last audible words being "moose" and "Indian"—the thought still intent on the scenes that had detained it so long.

He was buried, near his brother and sister, in "Sleepy Hollow," the quiet Concord burial-ground, close to the spot which became the grave of Nathaniel Hawthorne two years later. An address was given at the funeral by Emerson, a poem of Channing's was sung, and Thoreau's stanzas, "Sic Vita," were read by Alcott. "While we walked in procession up to the church," says one who was present,[4] "though the bell tolled the forty-four years he had numbered, we could not deem that *he* was dead whose ideas and sentiments were so vivid in our souls. As the fading image of pathetic clay lay before us, strewn with wild-flowers and forest sprigs, thoughts of its former occupant seemed blent with all the local landscapes. We still recall with emotion the tributary words so fitly spoken by friendly and illustrious lips. The hands of friends reverently lowered the body of the lonely poet into the bosom of the earth, on the pleasant hill-side of his native village, whose prospects will long wait to unfurl themselves to another observer so competent to discriminate their features, and so attuned to their moods." His grave was marked by a red stone, which bore no inscription but his name and date of death.[5]

Thoreau's collections of plants, Indian relics, and the like, were bequeathed by him to the Society of Natural History at Boston, of which he was an honorary member. The family business was carried on for some years after his death by his sister Sophia, who herself lived till 1876, having outlived her mother by four years. The last remaining member of the family was Miss Maria Thoreau, the sister of Thoreau's father, who died in Maine at an advanced age in 1881. But though the family is thus extinct in New England, the name of Thoreau is indelibly associated with the scenes amidst which he lived and died; and it has been well remarked that "the village of Concord is his monument, covered with suitable inscriptions by himself." A cairn of stones marks the site of the hut on the shore of Walden Pond, where the poet-naturalist spent the two most memorable years of his life, and wrote the greater part of his most memorable volume.[6]

"My greatest skill," says Thoreau himself, in words that might stand as his epitaph, "has been to want but little. For joy I could embrace the earth. I shall delight to be buried in it. And then I think of those amongst men who will know that I love them, though I tell them not." Truly there is a love that needs not telling—that is deepest and tenderest untold. And those who understand this love will understand the secret of Thoreau's story, and will never fail to own and reverence the sincerity and heroism of his life.

NOTES

1. See *Journal* for Feb. 8, 16, 23, 1857; also May 23, 1853, Dec. 31, 1851.

2. This was the ambrotype by Dunshee of New Bedford. See appendix: "Portraits of Thoreau."

3. Parker Pillsbury; whose account of the conversation is given in Mr. F. B. Sanborn's *Personality of Thoreau,* pp. 67–69.

4. W. R. Alger: *Solitudes of Nature and of Man.*

5. That stone is now gone. Its successor bears the names, and dates of birth and death, of every member of the family, except John, whose birthday no one could recall.

6. The cairn is said to be about ten yards from the actual site. The following is an extract from the journal of one of the many pilgrims who have since visited these scenes:—"A half-hour at Hawthorne's and Thoreau's graves. I got out and went up, of course, on foot, and stood a long while and pondered. They lie close together in a pleasant wooded spot well up the cemetery hill, 'Sleepy Hollow.' . . . Then to Walden Pond, that beautifully embower'd sheet of water, and spent over an hour there. On the spot in the woods where Thoreau had his solitary house is now quite a cairn of stones, to mark the place; I too carried one and deposited on the heap."—(Walt Whitman's *Specimen Days in America,* September 1881.) It is to be regretted that the Pond has now become a mere holiday resort.

9

Doctrines

A deliberate intent of advocating any particular class of doctrines is more than once disclaimed by Thoreau. He was an independent thinker, who put his theories into practice with unusual courage, and expressed himself in his books with unusual frankness, but he had no preconceived designs on the opinions of his fellowmen; he lived his life and said his say, and if he sought to exercise any influence on others, it was by no direct persuasion of argument or proselytism, but indirectly by the example of his own personality. He once asked a friend, who had entered the ministry, whether he had ever yet in preaching been "so fortunate as to say anything." On being answered in the affirmative, he remarked, "Then your preaching days are over. Can you bear to say it again?" By nature and temperament he was averse to any elaborate "system" of philosophy or ethics; he questioned everything, and would accept no philosophical formula for himself, nor offer any to his readers. This constitutional unwillingness to be trammelled by any tenet left its mark very distinctly both on the substance and the form of Thoreau's writings, and should be borne in mind when he is spoken of as the preacher of an ethical gospel; nevertheless, since he dwelt with much insistence on certain important truths, intellectual and moral, which are too generally overlooked, we are justified, with this reservation, in formulating as "doctrines" the views which he most frequently expressed.

We have already seen that he was before everything an idealist—his transcendentalism was not an adopted creed, but an innate habit of mind from which he never swerved, and which dominated all his philosophy. So far, it may be said, he did not differ to any remarkable degree from other idealists, who have all more or less recognised and followed the guiding light of the inner consciousness. But here we come to that distinctive quality which sets Thoreau on a separate footing from Emerson and other transcendentalist writers—the resolute practicalness which shows itself as clearly in his doctrines as in his actions. Though the ideal was always before him, he had no taste for the subtleties of mere metaphysical abstractions, but made a strong actuality the basis of his reasoning: there were thus two sides to his character and philosophy, the one the mystical and transcendental, which faced the boundless possibilities of the future, the other the practical and terrestrial, which was concerned with the realities of the present and the past.

It is true that these two qualities did not always work quite harmoniously together; for Thoreau was not careful to be systematic and verbally consistent; as he himself says, "How can I communicate with the gods, who am a pencil-maker on earth, and not be insane?" But, as a rule, the successful combination of common sense with transcendental sense is the characteristic feature of his doctrines; and this very dreamer and mystic who boasted that he built his castles in the air and then put the foundations under them, could also assert with equal truth, in another connection, that "it afforded him no satisfaction to commence to spring an arch before he had got a solid foundation." His philosophy of life is eminently keen-sighted, sound, and practical.

It has been asserted that Thoreau "is Emerson without domestic ties, or wish for them; save for a streak of benevolence, without those of humanity."[1] But this subordination of Thoreau as a mere pupil and follower of Emerson is not warranted by the facts of their relationship. The greater practicalness of Thoreau is frankly recognised by Emerson himself in a passage of his diary. "In reading Henry Thoreau's journal," he wrote, a year after his friend's death, "I am very sensible of the vigour of his constitution. That oaken strength which I noted whenever he walked or worked or surveyed wood-lots, the same unhesitating hand with which a field-labourer accosts a piece of work which I should shun as a waste of strength, he shows in his literary task. He has muscle, and ventures on and performs feats which I am forced to decline. In reading him I find the same thoughts, the same spirit that is in me, but he takes a step beyond and illustrates by excellent images that which I should have conveyed in a sleepy generalisation." "The resemblance of Thoreau to Emerson," says Mr. Conway, "was as superficial as that of a leaf-like creature to a leaf. Thoreau was quite as original as Emerson. He was not an imitator of any mortal; his thoughts and expressions are suggestions of a Thoreau-principle at work in the universe."[2]

This practical tendency in Thoreau was fostered and strengthened by his firm belief in the freedom of the human will. "I know of no more encouraging fact," he says, "than the unquestionable ability of man to elevate his life by a conscious endeavour." His religious and moral creed was founded on a fixed optimistic conviction that nature is working to some wise and benevolent end; joy was for him "the condition of life," and despondency nothing more than a senseless and idle aberration.

Inspired by this optimistic faith, Thoreau inculcates, more strongly perhaps than any other writer, a sense of content in one's own personality; he would have each individual develop quietly according to his own capacity and conditions. To waste no time in brooding over the past, but to live in the present, and nourish unbounded confidence in the future—this was the essence of his practical philosophy; and for support in this creed, and refreshment in the weaker moments of life, he looked to the unfailing health and beneficence, as he considered it, of wild nature.

This calm, optimistic nature-worship mainly determined Thoreau's attitude towards the religious sects, whose "snappish tenacity," and faint-hearted craving for external comfort and grace, were in direct contrast to his own absolute self-possession. "Really there is no infidelity nowadays," he wrote in *The Week,* "so great as that which prays, and keeps the Sabbath, and rebuilds the churches. The church is a sort of hospital for men's souls, and as full of quackery as the hospital for their bodies. Those who are taken into it live like pensioners in their Retreat or Sailors' Snug Harbour, where you may see a row of religious cripples sitting outside in sunny weather. Let not the apprehension that he may one day have to occupy a ward therein discourage the cheerful labours of the able-souled man." It may be imagined that the spirit of "defiant pantheism," as Horace Greeley called it, which breathes through all Thoreau's utterances on the subject of religion, and especially through the magnificent passage in the chapter on "Sunday" in *The Week,* must have caused him, and still causes him, to be mistrusted in so-called religious circles. It has been truly remarked of him that "he creates as much consternation among the saints as the sinners."

What, then, is the practical outcome of Thoreau's ethical teaching?

In the first place, he is an earnest and unwearied advocate of self-culture and self-respect, and insists again and again on the need of preserving our higher and nobler instincts from the contamination of what is base, trivial, and worldly; the body must be exercised into purity and vigour, and carefully safe-guarded against sloth, vice, and disease, and in like manner, from an intellectual point of view, the mind must be kept secure from the harmful and distracting influences of conventionality and gossip. The extreme delicacy of Thoreau's nature—a delicacy which was sensitive almost to fastidiousness—may be seen in the sharp and perhaps too arbitrary contrast which he sometimes draws between the spiritual and the animal instincts, and especially in the tone of his remarks on the subject of love. "The intercourse of the sexes," he says, "I have dreamed, is incredibly beautiful, too fair to be remembered. I have had thoughts about it, but they are among the most fleeting and irrecoverable in my experience. It is strange that men will talk of miracles, revelation, inspiration, and the like, as things past, while love remains. Some have asked if the stock of men could not be improved—if they could not be bred as cattle. Let Love be purified, and all the rest will follow. A pure love is thus indeed the panacea for all the ills of the world."

The eager self-seeking restlessness of modern society, with its ignorance or disregard of the claims of thoughtful repose, was summed up for Thoreau in the word "business." Nothing, in his opinion, not even crime, is so much opposed to the poetry of life as "business,"—it is a negation of life itself. Yet, as has already been said, the leisure which he advocated as essential to the well-being of every man was very different from idleness; indeed there have been few writers who, both in word and deed, have appraised the value of time more powerfully than Thoreau. If he rejected "business" in its commercial and money-making aspect, he none the less recognised that hard work is as important a discipline for the mind and morals as exercise is for the body, and that those who fail to support themselves by their own labour are doing a wrong both to themselves and others. For the same reason he urges on students and men of sedentary habits the advisability of taking a share in the simple common labours of everyday life, asserting that "the student who secures his coveted leisure and retirement by systematically shirking any labour necessary to man obtains but an ignoble and unprofitable leisure, defrauding himself of the experience which alone can make leisure fruitful."

We see, then, that Thoreau's first demand is for leisure and elbow-room, that each individual mind, instead of being crushed and warped in the struggle of life, may have space to develop its own distinctive qualities and follow the bent of its own natural temperament. Never has there lived a more determined and unalterable individualist. Everything, according to his maxims, must be examined; nothing must be taken on trust; he was, as Emerson calls him, "a protestant *à l'outrance,*" and unhesitatingly rejected many customs which are supposed to have the sanction of experience and tradition. He declared that after living some thirty years on this planet he had yet to hear a word of valuable advice from his elders. When a young man of his acquaintance professed a desire to adopt his mode of life, his answer was that he would have each one find out and pursue *his own* way, and not that of his father or his neighbour.

It must not be supposed, however, that he wholly ignored the possibility of wise co-operation—on the contrary, he expressly states in *Walden,* when advocating the adoption of a better system of village education, that "to act collectively is according to the spirit of our institutions;" and in the account of his Canadian tour, when he describes the machine-like regularity with which the troops at Montreal went through their drill in the Champ de Mars, he exclaims that a true co-operation and harmony might be possible, "if men could combine thus earnestly and patiently and harmoniously to some really worthy end." But this seems to have been nothing more than a distant anticipation; under present conditions he considered that the best hope of society lay in the progress and gradual perfecting of the individual man by his own personal effort. At a time when Fourier's doctrines had obtained great hold in New England, and when various schemes of co-operative associations, by which society was to be entirely reorganised and regenerated, were being eagerly discussed, it was inevitable that so shrewd and practical a thinker as Thoreau should—in spite of his idealism—fall back more and more on what he considered the solid basis of individual independence. This view is stated very clearly in his criticism of a volume entitled *The Paradise within the Reach of All Men,* in which the magical results of co-operation had been depicted in glowing colours—

> Alas! this is the crying sin of the age, this want of faith in the prevalence of a man. Nothing can be effected but by one man. He

> who wants help wants everything. True, this is the condition of our weakness, but it can never be the means of our recovery. We must first succeed alone, that we may enjoy our success together. We trust that the social movements which we witness indicate an aspiration not to be thus cheaply satisfied. In this matter of reforming the world we have little faith in corporations; not thus was it first formed.[3]

Closely connected with this strong individualism are Thoreau's anarchist doctrines. He regards all established government as, at best, a necessary evil, which we must tolerate as we can during the present transitional phase of human society, in the belief that the ultimate condition of mankind will be, like the primitive, one of individual liberty. Politics he set aside as "unreal, incredible, and insignificant." "Blessed are the young," was his new version of the Beatitudes, "for they do not read the President's Message." For the same reasons he expressed a strong dislike of the general tone of the American press, which he considered, with a few exceptions, to be venal and time-serving. In at least two of his essays, the "Plea for Captain John Brown" and "Slavery in Massachusetts," this feeling finds an outlet in a fierce philippic against the hireling journals which did not scruple to use their utmost influence in the service of the slave-holding party.

Yet here too, as elsewhere, there is a danger of exaggerating the extent of Thoreau's lack of sympathy with contemporary modes of thought. It is true he preaches anarchism and civil disobedience; yet, under a rough exterior, he loved his country well, and in his peculiar way was perhaps as patriotic a citizen as any to be found in Massachusetts. He admits that the American Government, though not an ideal one, is good enough when viewed from a lower than the ideal standpoint, and more than once expresses his own desire to be a peaceable and law-abiding citizen. Moreover, in spite of his contempt for politics and politicians, he does not deny that "countless reforms are called for," and shows that he is aware that the condition of the working classes is destined to be the paramount question of the age. But all his social doctrines point finally to this end—that the path must be left clear for the free development of individual character.

"There will never be a really free and enlightened State," he says in his essay on "Civil Disobedience,"

> until the State comes to recognise the individual as a higher and independent power, from which all its own power and authority are derived, and treats him accordingly. I please myself with imagining a State at last which can afford to be just to all men, and to treat the individual with respect as a neighbour; which even would not think it inconsistent with its own repose, if a few were to live aloof from it, not meddling with it, nor embraced by it, who fulfilled all the duties of neighbours and fellow-men. A State which bore this kind of fruit, and suffered it to drop off as fast as it ripened, would prepare the way for a still more perfect and glorious State, which also I have imagined, but not yet anywhere seen.

Society then is to be reformed, according to Thoreau's doctrine, by individual effort, and the gospel which he preaches to the individual is that of simplicity. Simplification of life (by which is meant a questioning, and perhaps rejection, of the various artificial "comforts" and luxuries, and a dependence only on the actual necessaries—food, shelter, clothing, and fuel) is frequently advocated by Thoreau, from his own practical experience, as lending strength, courage, and self-reliance to the individual character, and so, in proportion to the extent of its practice, to the State.

It must be repeated that this doctrine, however strange and unpalatable it may be to the popular mood, is not that of an ascetic. The simplicity which Thoreau inculcates does not, like asceticism, renounce the luxuries of life by way of a religious penance, but because it is convinced that life on the whole, is healthier and happier without them. What he urges is not that men should deny themselves certain comforts while they still believe them to be comforts, but that in each case they should test the truth by practical experience, and not continue to regard as necessaries many things which a day's trial would prove to be superfluous and perhaps actually harmful. This distinction between a natural taste and an acquired habit is a vital one, yet it is generally overlooked by the opponents of Thoreau's philosophy. He laughs at the absurdity of those writers who talk of the usefulness of "artificial wants" in drawing out the resources of nature, since every artificial want must of necessity bring with it its own Nemesis of proportionally increased toil; whereas, on the contrary, the practice of hardihood and frugality is productive of health, independence, and restfulness both to body and mind. In a word, the simplicity which he preaches is based not on the repression, but rather on the better gratification, of the true pleasures of existence. Which is the more enjoyable to indulge—the spiritual instinct or the sensual? Let each man make his own choice; but let him at least be sure that he *is* really following his own tastes, and not merely conforming to the dictates of custom and tradition.

The charge often made against Thoreau, that he is in opposition to the course of modern progress, and prefers savagery to civilisation, is only tenable on a very short-sighted and perfunctory view of the meaning of his gospel. He himself notes in his diary that his lectures used to call forth such inquiries as "Would you have us return to the savage state?"—a misconception of his meaning which was doubtless rendered more general by his brevity of speech, epigrammatic tone, and characteristic unwillingness to explain himself. But a careful study of his writings as a whole, and of *Walden* in particular, can leave us in no doubt as to his true position on this point. He expressly states his belief that civilisation is a real advance in the condition of mankind, and that the farmer displaces the Indian "because he redeems the meadow, and so makes himself stronger and in some respects more natural." But, while making this admission, he points out what is too often overlooked by comfortable statisticians, that, though the majority of civilised men are better situated than the savage, there is a minority which is not so. He asserts, then, that the problem to which we should apply ourselves is how "to combine the hardiness of the savage with the intellectualness of the civilised man." When he inveighs against the numerous follies, and defects, and diseases observable in civilisation, he does so, not because he doubts or denies its superiority to the savage state, but because (to quote his own words) he wishes "to show at what a sacrifice this advantage is at present obtained, and to suggest that we may possibly so live as to secure all the advantage without suffering any of the disadvantage."

In the same connection it should be noted that Thoreau exhibits no reactionary feeling against the strides made by science and modern mechanical invention, however strongly he may protest against the unnecessary desecration of natural scenery. He descants on the enterprise, courage, and alertness of commerce, which goes steadily on its path undismayed and unhindered by the obstacles of climate and season, and declares that it cheered him in his Walden hermitage when he heard the train rattle past each morning on its road to Boston. All he desiderates is a worthier object as the end and aim of so much toil and industry. Nor was he, as some have supposed, an enemy to art, though he may have been, as Emerson says, "insensible to some fine traits of culture." He did not wish to banish ornament from our dwellings, except such as is external and superficial, a mere conventional and fashionable appendage, instead of what it should be, a simple and natural growth.

It may here be worth while to inquire how far these principles of individualism and simplicity were meant by Thoreau to be applied, and how far they were rightly applicable, to the social question of his time. There is no indication whatever in any of his writings that he intended his doctrines to be understood, directly and literally, as containing a panacea for human ills; he did not wish his fellow-beings to leave their towns and villages in order to live in shanties, nor was he under the impression, as some of his critics would have us believe, that the inhabitants of crowded cities were free to march out and live in blissful seclusion in some neighbouring wood. Thoreau, whatever the limitations of his genius may have been, was a shrewd and clear-sighted man; and if any of his readers find themselves attributing to him such ineptitudes as those just mentioned, they may feel assured that the misunderstanding is on their own side, and that by lack of sympathy they have failed to grasp his true meaning. It should be remembered that he wrote primarily and immediately for his own fellow-citizens of Concord and a limited New England audience; and further, that the social problem was far less difficult and complex at that time in New England than it is now after a lapse of fifty years. Extreme poverty was a rare exception and not a normal condition among the peasantry of Concord; there was more elbow-room and opportunity for individual effort, so that an example such as that set by Thoreau was not by any means the impossibility which it might have been elsewhere. As a matter of fact, he seldom recommended his own way of living to his neighbours or fellow-townsmen, being convinced that each man must shape his own career; and insofar as he addressed his doctrines to the general public, it was distinctly not with the intent of persuading them to live as he did, but in the hope of stimulating independent thought, and of drawing attention to those simple commonsense principles without which there can be no lasting health or contentment either for individual or community.

Mr. R. L. Stevenson has remarked of Thoreau that in his whole works one can find no trace of pity. If it were possible at all to maintain this assertion, it could only be in the limited sense that he dwells usually on the iniquity of the wrong-doer rather than on the feelings of the sufferer; he does not, for instance, *express* his pity for the slave (though we know from the accounts already quoted how strong his pity was), but he shows it in a more practical form by his attitude towards the slave-holder. It is true that, with his characteristic dislike of system, he disclaims any distinct theory of compassion, while his optimistic belief in the beneficence of nature prevents him from repining at the mere existence of suffering and wrong. Nevertheless, Thoreau is himself one of the humanest of writers, and has contributed to the literature of humanitarianism some of its most striking protests. His detestation of war was shown in his refusal to pay the poll-tax at the time when the United States made an unjustifiable attack on Mexico. He declares fighting to be "a damnable business," and at variance with the will and conscience of those compelled to engage in it—"soldiers, colonel, captain, corporal, powder-monkeys, and all," and elsewhere he asks: "Will it not be thought disreputable at length, as duelling between individuals now is?" Of his opinions concerning slaveholding it is not necessary to say more; but there is a remarkable saying of his about John Brown which deserves to be quoted in this connection. Noting the fact that Brown had not received a college education, but had studied Liberty in "the great University of the West," he adds: "Such were his *humanities,* and not any study of grammar. He would have left a Greek accent slanting the wrong way, and righted up a falling man." It would be well if all our professors and students of *literæ humaniores* would lay this admirable sentiment to heart.

Humanity to animals was one of the most conspicuous virtues in Thoreau's character, and is constantly, if indirectly, advocated in his writings. His conception of the animal races has been described as "a sort of mystic evolution." Thus he regards the foxes as "rudimental burrowing men, still standing on their defence, awaiting their transformation;" while the dog is to the fox as the white man to the red. The horse appears to him as a human being in a humble state of existence, and the human way in which the oxen behave when loosed from the yoke at evening affects him pathetically. The wild shaggy moose in the Maine forests are "moose-men, clad in a sort of Vermont gray or homespun," and he expresses respect even for the skunk, for its suggested resemblance to one of the human aborigines of the country. Individuality is recognised and respected by him in the non-human no less than the human races; he complains of man's "not educating the horse, not trying to develop his nature, but merely getting work out of him." It was this sense of brotherhood, as I have already remarked, which gave Thoreau his extraordinary power over beasts and birds; and his singular humanity to animals is due to the same source. During the greater part of his life he was a vegetarian in practice, and in several passages has made profession of his faith in the humanities of diet.[4]

His position as a naturalist was strongly influenced by the same humane sentiments. His methods were not those of the anatomist and man of science; he held that "nature must be viewed humanly to be viewed at all, that is, her scenes must be associated with humane affections;" she was to him a living entity, to be loved and reverenced, and not a subject for cold and unimpassioned observation. Accordingly, in his remarks on nature and natural history there is a decided prevalence of that peculiarly introspective and moralising mood, characteristic of the poet-naturalist as distinct from the scientist, which seeks to transmute the mere facts and results of external observation into symbolical thoughts and images which may illustrate the life of man. It is this human self-consciousness that differentiates Thoreau from the naturalist and observer pure and simple, such as Gilbert White.

It has been remarked by Mr. John Burroughs that it was supernatural rather than natural history that Thoreau studied, and that he made no discoveries of importance in the scientific field because he looked *through* nature instead of *at* her, and was "more intent on the natural history of his own thought than on that of the bird." His observations, however, are not the less important because they differ from those acquired by the ordinary method; on the contrary, they are more valuable on that account, inasmuch as the poet is higher and rarer than the naturalist. Nathaniel Hawthorne has recorded how Thoreau was enabled by this inner faculty to see the water-lily as few others could see it; "he has beheld beds of them unfolding in due succession as the sunrise stole gradually from flower to flower—a sight not to be hoped for, unless when a poet adjusts his inward eye to a proper focus with the outward organ." This idealist quality constitutes the peculiar property of Thoreau's teaching on the subject of nature; but that it did not disqualify him from doing good service as a scientific observer may be gathered from the remarkable tribute which has been paid to him by one of Darwin's interpreters:—

> Like no one else, he knew the meaning of every note and movement of bird and beast, and fish and insect. Born out of due time, just too early for the great change in men's views of nature which transferred all interest in outer life from the mere dead things one sees in museums to their native habits and modes of living, he was yet in some sort a vague and mystical anticipatory precursor of the modern school of functional biologists. . . . Page after page of his diary notes facts about the pollen showers of pine-trees, the fertilisation of skunk-cabbage, the nesting of birds, the preferences of mink or musk-rat, the courtship of butterflies, all of a piece with those minute observations on which naturalists nowadays build their most interesting theories.[5]

The conclusion of our view of Thoreau's doctrines thus brings us back to the contention with which we started. He was an idealist who looked through the outer husk and surface of life, and saw the true reality in what to most men is but a vision and a dream. He had in large measure what Emerson calls "the philosopher's perception of identity"; the phenomena of time and space did not affect him—Walden Pond was to him an Atlantic Ocean, a moment was eternity. The means on which he relies for the correction of popular delusions are the independence of the individual mind, and those simple, practical modes of living which alone can keep a man independent. Finally, for all his asperity of tone in the reproof of what he considered to be blameworthy, he was a firm believer in the gradual progress and ultimate renovation of mankind, being convinced that improvement is "the only excuse for reproduction." It was no cynical or misanthropic faith that found expression in his writings.

NOTES

1. Professor Nichol's *American Literature.*
2. *Emerson at Home and Abroad.*
3. *Democratic Review,* November 1843.
4. "Left to my chosen pursuits, I should never drink tea nor coffee, nor eat meat." *Journal,* Dec. 18, 1853.

"Whatever my own practice may be, I have no doubt that it is a part of the destiny of the human race, in its gradual improvement, to leave off eating animals, as surely as the savage tribes have left off eating each other when they came in contact with the more civilised." *Walden.*

5. Grant Allen, *Fortnightly Review,* May 1888.

10

Writings

The lack of system which is noticeable in Thoreau's character may be traced in the style of his writings as plainly as in his philosophical views. He was not careful as to the outer form and finish of his works, for he believed that the mere literary contour is of quite secondary importance in comparison with the inner spirit; let the worthiness of the latter once be assured, and the former will fall naturally into its proper shape. Furthermore, although, as we have seen, writing was more and more recognised by him as his profession in his later years, he was at all times conscious of a fuller and higher calling than that of the literary man—as he valued nature before art, so he valued life before literature. He both preached and practised a combination of literary work and manual; of the pen and of the spade; of the study and of the open sky. He protested against that tendency in our civilisation which carries division of labour to such an extent that the student is deprived of healthy out-door work, while the labourer is deprived of opportunity for self-culture. He imagines the case of some literary professor, who sits in his library writing a treatise on the huckleberry, while hired huckleberry-pickers and cooks are engaged in the task of preparing him a pudding of the berries. A book written under such conditions will be worthless. "There will be none of the spirit of the huckleberry in it. I believe in a different kind of division of labour, and that the professor should divide himself between the library and the huckleberry field." His opinions on the subject of literary style are clearly stated in *The Week,* and are no doubt in great measure a record of his own practice:

> Can there be any greater reproach than an idle learning? Learn to split wood at least. The necessity of labour and conversation with many men and things to the scholar is rarely well remembered; steady labour with the hands, which engrosses the attention also, is unquestionably the best method of removing palaver and sentimentality out of one's style, both of speaking and writing. If he has worked hard from morning till night, though he may have grieved that he could not be watching the train of his thoughts during that time, yet the few hasty lines which at evening record his day's experience will be more musical and true than his freest but idle fancy could have furnished. Surely the writer is to address a world of labourers, and such therefore must be his own discipline. He will not idly dance at his work who has wood to cut and cord before nightfall in the short days of winter, but every stroke will be husbanded, and ring soberly through the wood; and so will the strokes of that scholar's pen, which at evening record the story of the day, ring soberly, yet cheerily, on the ear of the reader, long after the echoes of his axe have died away.

Such were, in fact, the conditions under which Thoreau wrote many of the pages of the journal from which his own essays were constructed; and, whatever may be thought of his general principle, there can be no doubt that in his particular case the result was very felicitous. It was his pleasure and his determination that his writing should be redolent of the open-air scenery by which it was primarily inspired. "I trust," he says of *The Week* (and the same may be said of all his volumes), "it does not smell so much of the study and library, even of the poet's attic, as of the fields and woods; that it is a hypæthral or unroofed book, lying open under the ether, and permeated by it, open to all weathers, not easy to be kept on a shelf." In this way Thoreau added a new flavour to literature by the unstudied freshness and wildness of his tone, and succeeded best where he made least effort to be successful. "It is only out of the fulness of thinking," says Stevenson, "that expression drops perfect like a ripe fruit; and when Thoreau wrote so nonchalantly at his desk, it was because he had been vigorously active during his walk." Even Lowell, a far less friendly critic, is compelled, on this point, to express his admiration. "With every exception, there is no writing comparable with Thoreau's in kind that is comparable with it in degree, where it is best.

His range was narrow, but to be a master is to be a master. There are sentences of his as perfect as anything in the language, and thoughts as clearly crystallised; his metaphors and images are always fresh from the soil."

This success, although naturally and unconsciously attained, had of course been rendered possible in the first instance by an honest course of study; for Thoreau, like every other master of literary expression, had passed through his strict apprenticeship. Though comparatively indifferent to modern languages, he was familiar with the best classical writers of Greece and Rome, and his style was partly formed on models drawn from one of the great eras in English literature, the post-Elizabethan period. It is a noticeable fact that "mother-tongue" was a word which he loved to use even in his college days; and the homely vigour of his own writings was largely due to the industry with which he had laboured in these quiet but fertile fields. Nor must it be supposed, because he did not elaborate his work according to the usual canons, that he was a careless or indolent writer—on the contrary, it was his habit to correct his manuscripts with unfailing diligence. His sincerity showed itself as clearly in the style of his writing as in the manner of his life. "The one great rule of composition—and if I were a professor of rhetoric I should insist on this—is to *speak the truth.* This first, this second, this third."

In his choice of subjects it was the common that most often enlisted his sympathy and attention. "The theme," he says, "is nothing; the life is everything. Give me simple, cheap, and homely themes. I omit the unusual—the hurricanes and earthquakes, and describe the common. This has the greatest charm, and is the true theme of poetry. Give me the obscure life, the cottage of the poor and humble, the work-days of the world, the barren fields."

Numerous passages might be quoted from Thoreau's works which exhibit these picturesque and suggestive qualities. He had a poet's eye for all forms of beauty, moral and material alike, and for the subtle analogies that exist between the one class and the other—in a word, he was possessed of a most vivid and quickening imagination. His images and metaphors are bold, novel, and impressive—as when, to take but a couple of instances, he alludes to the lost anchors of vessels wrecked off the coast of Cape Cod as "the sunken faith and hope of mariners, to which they trusted in vain;" or describes the autumnal warmth on the sheltered side of Walden as "the still glowing embers which the summer, like a departing hunter, had left." And, with all his simplicity and directness of speech, he has an unconscious, almost mystic, eloquence which stamps him unmistakably as an inspired writer, a man of true and rare genius; so that it has been well said of him that "he lived and died to transfuse external nature into human words." In this respect his position among prose-writers is unique; no one, unless it be Richard Jefferies, can be placed in the same category with him.

Insofar as he studied the external form of his writings, the aim and object which Thoreau set before him may be summed up in one word—concentration. He avows his delight in sentences which are "concentrated and nutty." The secret of his own literary style could not have been more accurately described. The brief, barbed, epigrammatic sentences which bristle throughout his writings, pungent with shrewd wisdom and humour, are the appropriate expression of his keen thrifty nature; there is not a superfluous word or syllable, but each passage goes straight to the mark, and tells its tale, as the work of a man who has some more urgent duty to perform than to adorn his pages with artificial tropes and embellishments. He is fond of surprising and challenging his readers by the piquancy and strangeness of his sayings, and his use of paradox is partly due to the same desire to stimulate and awaken curiosity, partly to his wayward and contradictory nature. The dangers and demerits of a paradoxical style are sufficiently obvious; and no writer has ever been less careful than Thoreau to safeguard himself against misunderstandings on this score.[1] He has consequently been much misunderstood, and will always be so, save where the reader brings to his task a certain amount of sympathy and kindred sense of humour.

To those who are not gifted with the same sense of the inner identity which links together many things that are externally unlike, some of Thoreau's thoughts and sayings must necessarily appear to be a fair subject for ridicule. Yet that he should have been charged with possessing no "humour" would be inexplicable, save for the fact that the definitions of that quality are so various and so vague. Broad wit and mirthful geniality he certainly had not, and he confessedly disliked writings in which there is a conscious and deliberate attempt to be amusing. He found Rabelais, for instance, intolerable; "it may be sport to him," he says, "but it is death to us; a mere humorist, indeed, is a most unhappy man, and his readers are most unhappy also." But though he would not or could not recognise humour as a distinct and independent quality, and even attempted, as we are told, to eliminate what he considered "levity" from some of his essays, he none the less enjoyed keenly—and himself unmistakably exhibited—the quiet, latent, unobtrusive humour which is one of the wholesome and saving principles of human life. Among Thoreau's own writings, *Walden* is especially pervaded by this subtle sense of humour, grave, dry, pithy, sententious, almost saturnine in its tone, yet perhaps for that very reason the more racy and suggestive to those readers who have the faculty for appreciating it.

He could not, as his friend Channing observes, "mosaic" his essays, but preferred to give himself free play by throwing them into the narrative and autobiographical form. *The Week* and *Walden,* the two volumes which were published in his lifetime, are both framed on this principle, a more or less slight record of personal experience being made the peg on which to hang a great deal of ethical speculation. Apart from all question of the value of the opinions advanced, the charm of those books lies mainly in their intellectual alertness, keen spiritual insight, and brilliant touches of picturesque description. Few authors have created such a rich store of terse felicitous sayings, or have drawn such vivid and sympathetic sketches of natural scenery. Numerous examples of his laconic incisive utterances have already been incidentally quoted. Here is a characteristic open-air picture of a bright breezy day on the Concord river, where he spent so much of his time—

> Many waves are there agitated by the wind, keeping nature fresh, the spray blowing in your face, reeds and rushes waving; ducks by the hundred, all uneasy in the surf, in the raw wind, just ready to rise, and now going off with a clatter and a whistling like riggers straight for Labrador, flying against the stiff gale with reefed wings, or else circling round first with all their paddles briskly moving, just over the surf, to reconnoitre you before they leave these parts; gulls wheeling overhead; musk-rats swimming for dear life, wet and cold, with no fire to warm them by that you know of, their laboured homes rising here and there like haystacks; and countless mice and moles and winged titmice along the sunny windy shore; cranberries tossed on the waves and heaving up on the beach, their little red skiffs beating about among the alders;—such healthy natural tumult as proves the last day is not yet at hand. And there stand all around the alders and birches

and oaks and maples full of glee and sap, holding in their buds until the waters subside.

Here, too, to show the more human side of Thoreau's genius, is one of the picturesque character-sketches which are far from uncommon in his writings—

> I can just remember an old brown-coated man who was the Walton of this stream, who had come over from Newcastle, England, with his son—the latter a stout and hearty man who had lifted an anchor in his day. A straight old man he was, who took his way in silence through the meadows, having passed the period of communication with his fellows; his old experienced coat, hanging long and straight and brown as the yellow-pine bark, glittering with so much smothered sunlight, if you stood near enough, no work of art but naturalised at length. I often discovered him unexpectedly amid the pads and the gray willows when he moved, fishing in some old country method—for youth and age then went a-fishing together—full of incommunicable thoughts, perchance about his own Tyne and Northumberland. He was always to be seen in serene afternoons haunting the river, and almost rustling with the sedge; so many sunny hours in an old man's life, entrapping silly fish; almost grown to be the sun's familiar; what need had he of hat or raiment any, having served out his time, and seen through such thin disguises. I have seen how his coeval fates rewarded him with the yellow perch, and yet I thought his luck was not in proportion to his years; and I have seen when, with slow steps and weighed down with aged thoughts, he disappeared with his fish under his low-roofed house on the skirts of the village. I think nobody else saw him; nobody else remembers him now, for he soon after died, and migrated to new Tyne streams. His fishing was not a sport, not solely a means of subsistence, but a sort of solemn sacrament and withdrawal from the world, just as the aged read their Bibles.

Those of Thoreau's shorter essays which deal with natural history and outdoor life are to be found reprinted in his *Excursions,* a volume published the year after his death, with the well-known prefatory memoir by Emerson. There is a wild, racy, indefinable charm about them which is all their own; they are by no means well "finished" and rounded off, when viewed from an artistic—or shall we say artificial—standpoint; for Thoreau, with all his conciseness in form, loves to gossip on without regard to the laws of essay-writing, and will not deny himself the pleasure of quoting largely, when the whim takes him, from his favourite poets, or from the old prose chroniclers who wrote of the places which he visited. Yet the final effect is altogether delightful; and no reader who has once caught and appreciated the rare mystic flavour of these wildlings of literature could ever regret that they were not subjected to the conventional pruning. They can no more be taken to the literary market and weighed in the critical balance than their prototype the "wild apple," which furnished Thoreau with some of his choicest themes.

The "Anti-Slavery and Reform Papers," which are now included in the *Miscellanies,* are more direct and didactic in aim than the *Excursions.* Some of Thoreau's most brilliant and pungent sayings are to be found in these essays, of which the very best are the "Plea for John Brown," the most impassioned of all his writings, and "Life without Principle," which conveys in brief form the substance of his protest against the follies of modern society.

The original source which provided material for his essays and volumes was the daily journal, which was kept by Thoreau with great fulness and regularity from 1837, the year when he left college, to a short time before his death in 1862, and amounted in all to no less than thirty large volumes.

We have seen, in the story of Thoreau's life, how his daily walks were not, as with most men, a time of leisure and recreation, but an essential part of his day's work and of his duties as poet-naturalist. He went to hill-top, or forest, or swamp, or river-bank, not as an aimless wanderer seeking to while away an afternoon, but as an inspector going his rounds; and he paid his visits deliberately and on principle to such animals, birds, nests, trees, or flowers as he happened to have under observation. He took notes on the spot, even when he walked, as was frequently the case, in the night-time; and on his return home he expanded these notes into graphic descriptions, interspersed with appropriate meditations, which sometimes, in the earlier volumes of the journal, took the form of verse. His notes on natural history constitute the larger portion of the entries.

From this journal Thoreau drew freely when preparing his essays or lectures, as the case might be; but, before being given to the world, every passage and sentence underwent further careful revision. After his death the unpublished manuscripts and diaries remained for fourteen years in the charge of his sister Sophia, who, at her death in 1876, bequeathed them to her brother's friend and correspondent, Mr. Blake.[2] Portions of the journal were edited by Mr. Blake in four volumes, under the titles of *Early Spring in Massachusetts, Summer, Autumn,* and *Winter,* various passages, written in different years, being grouped together according to the days on which they were written, so as to give a connected picture of the seasons; but it was not until the issue of the "Walden" edition of Thoreau's writings, in 1906, that the Journal was published in its entirety.

A volume of Thoreau's *Letters* was edited by Emerson in 1865. The letters included are, as a rule, much more severely transcendental in tone than the essays and diaries—"abominably didactic," Channing called them—and their seriousness is seldom relieved by the keen humour of *Walden.* It seems that Emerson, in selecting them, made it his object to exhibit a "perfect piece of stoicism," and therefore inserted only a few of the domestic letters, which showed the other and tenderer side of Thoreau's character—an arrangement which was justly described by Sophia Thoreau as not quite fair to her brother. This one-sided impression has now been corrected by the volume of *Familiar Letters,* edited by Mr. Sanborn in 1894, which gives a far wider and fairer idea of the scope of Thoreau's character.

Last in the list of Thoreau's writings there remains to be considered his poetry. Strictly speaking, he can hardly be called a poet at all, for, though he had a large gift of the poetic inspiration, he lacked the lyrical fire and melodious utterance which are at least equally indispensable to the creation of a true poem; his verses are therefore interesting less for their own intrinsic value than for the light they indirectly throw on his personality and genius. The description which Emerson gave of his own poetic talent may be applied *totidem verbis* to that of Thoreau. "I am born a poet—of a low class without a doubt, yet a poet. My singing, be sure, is very husky, and is for the most part in prose. Still, I am a poet in the sense of a perceiver and dear lover of the harmonies that are in the soul and in matter, and specially of the correspondence between these and those."

Thoreau's poems were mostly written from 1837 to 1847, when he was between twenty and thirty years of age. It was his method to jot down in his journal a stanza or two from time to time, and afterwards to combine these scattered pieces into a connected poem, each verse of which would thus be brief, pointed, and sententious. He had been strongly influenced by his early readings in the seventeenth-century school, and the resemblance in his style to that of Herbert, Cowley, and other writers of that era is very striking, his poetry being of the same "gnomic" order, abounding in quaint conceits, thrifty maxims, and elaborate antitheses, with here and there a dainty stanza or series of stanzas, marked by deep insight and felicitous expression. His idea of the poet's vocation is characteristic. The poet is "no tender slip of fairy stock, but the toughest son of earth and heaven, and by his greater strength and endurance his fainting companions will recognise the god in him. He will hit the nail on the head, and we shall not know the strength of his hammer." Thus in his poems he is less the artist than the moralist; but the delicacy and nobility of the thought often lift the rough unpolished lines out of the region of commonplace, and make them pleasing and memorable.

Many of Thoreau's early poems found publication in the *Dial,* and met with much ridicule in critical and anti-transcendental circles; we are told that an unquenchable laughter, "like that of the gods at Vulcan's limping, went up over his ragged and halting lines." He afterwards included some of these pieces in *The Week* and other prose volumes, preferring, after the discontinuance of the *Dial,* not to publish them separately, but "as choruses or hymns or word-pictures, to illustrate the movement of his thought." He told a friend during his last illness that he had destroyed many of his verses because Emerson did not praise them, an act which he afterwards regretted. A large number of Thoreau's poems may be found in *The Week,* and a few were reprinted by Emerson in an appendix to the volume of *Letters;* but the first collection that can at all claim to be a representative one is that published in 1895 under the title of *Poems of Nature.*

The final conclusion of the reader will probably be that the best poetry of Thoreau's nature found expression in his prose. "Great prose of equal elevation," he thinks, "commands our respect more than great verse, since it implies a more permanent and level height, and a life pervaded with the grandeur of the thought. The poet only makes an irruption, like a Parthian, and is off again, shooting while he retreats; but the prose writer has conquered, like a Roman, and settled colonies."

NOTES

1. His comments on his own faults of style—"paradoxes," "playing with words," etc.—may be seen in the *Journal,* Sept. 3, 1854.

2. Soon after Thoreau's death there was talk of publishing the complete journal, but Sophia Thoreau could not make up her mind to it, and the plan was dropped. In 1866 she wrote to a friend: "These papers are very sacred to me, and I feel inclined to defer giving them to the public for the present."

11

Conclusion

Thus, as we have seen, the most vigorous protest ever raised against that artificiality in life and literature which is one of the chief dangers of our complex civilisation, proceeded not from some sleepy old-world province, which might have been expected to be unable to keep pace with a progressive age, but from the heart of the busiest and most advanced nation on the globe—it is to Yankeeland that we owe the example and the teaching of the "Bachelor of Nature." The personality of Thoreau is so singular and so unique that it seems useless to attempt, as some have done, to draw out any elaborate parallel between his character and that of other reformers, who have protested against some prevalent tendency in the age in which they lived. Those who are interested in seeking for literary prototypes may perhaps, in this case, find one in Abraham Cowley, a member of that school of gnomic poets with which Thoreau was so familiar, and moreover a zealous lover of the peace and solitude of nature. He lived in close retirement during the later years of his life, and his death, which, like Thoreau's, was due to a cold caught while he was botanising, is attributed by his biographer to "his very delight in the country and the fields, which he had long fancied above all other pleasures." Some of Cowley's remarks in his essays on solitude are conceived in a spirit very similar to that of Thoreau. "The First Minister of State," he says, "has not so much business in public as a wise man in private; if the one has little leisure to be alone, the other has less leisure to be in company; the one has but part of the affairs of one nation, the other all the works of God and nature under his consideration;" and elsewhere he expresses the wish that men could "unravel all they have woven, that we might have our woods and our innocence again, instead of our castles and our policies." But these parallels, between two men of widely different periods and purposes, can contain nothing more than slight and superficial resemblances. Nor, except for his general connection with Emerson and the transcendentalists, is it more easy to match Thoreau with any ethical writer of his own generation.

As a "poet-naturalist," however, Thoreau is distinctly akin to Richard Jefferies and other writers of that school. Jefferies' character was richer and more sensuous than Thoreau's, but they had the same mystic temperament, the same impatience of tradition and conventionality, the same passionate love of woods and fields and streams, and the same gift of brilliant language in which to record their observations. It is curious to compare these modern devotees of country life with the old-fashioned naturalists of whom Izaak Walton and Gilbert White are the most illustrious examples. While the honest old angler prattles on contentedly, like the babbling streams by which he spent his days, with here and there a pious reflection on the beneficence of Providence and the adaptation of means to ends, and while the kindly naturalist of Selborne devotes himself absolutely and unreservedly to the work of chronicling the fauna and flora of the district about which he writes, these later authors have brought to the treatment of similar subjects a far deeper insight into the beauty and pathos of nature, and a power of poetical description which was not dreamed of by their simple yet not less devoted predecessors. It is mainly to Thoreau in America, and to Jefferies in England, that we owe the recognition and study of what may be called the poetry of natural history—a style of thought and writing which is peculiar to the last thirty or forty years. The study of nature has, of course, been from time immemorial one of the great subjects of poetry, but, so far, it was nature in its more general aspects; it was not till comparatively recent years that there was discovered to be poetry also in the accurate and patient observation of natural phenomena. We have now learnt that natural history, which was formerly regarded as a grave and meritorious study of a distinctly prosaic kind, may be made to yield material for the most imaginative and poetical reflections.

When Thoreau died in 1862, Richard Jefferies was a boy of fourteen, busily engaged among his native Wiltshire Downs in laying the foundation of his wonderful knowledge of outdoor life. There is no mention of Thoreau in his writings, nor any indication that he had read him; yet one is often struck by suggestive resemblances in their manner of thought. Take, for instance, that half-serious, half-whimsical contention of Thoreau's, which has probably been more misunderstood than any other of his sayings—that Concord, in its natural features, contains all the phenomena that travellers have noted elsewhere—and compare it with the following opinion expressed by Jefferies:—"It has long been one of my fancies that this country is an epitome of the natural world, and that if any one has come really into contact with its productions, and is familiar with them, and what they mean and represent, then he has a knowledge of all that exists on the earth." In reading these words, one has a difficulty in remembering that they were not written by Thoreau.

The association of Thoreau's name with the district in which he lived and died is likely to become closer and closer as the years go on. Great nature-lovers, it has been truly remarked, have the faculty of stamping the impress of their own character on whole regions of country, so that there are certain places which belong by indisputable right to certain persons who have made them peculiarly and perpetually their own. As the Lake District is inseparably connected with the names of the poets who dwelt and wrote there; as the Scotch border-land owes close allegiance to Scott, and the Ayrshire fields to Burns; and as the little Hampshire village of Selborne is the inalienable property of Gilbert White—so the thoughts of those who visit Concord turn inevitably to Thoreau. "Thoreau's affections and genius," says one of his admirers, "were so indissolubly bound up with this country that now he is gone he presents himself to my mind as one of these local genii or deified men whom the Scandinavian mythology gave as guardians to the northern coasts and mountains. These beings kept off murrain from the cattle and sickness from men. They made the nights sweet and salubrious, and the days productive. If Thoreau had lived in the early ages of Greece, he would have taken his place in the popular imagination along with his favourite god Pan."

That a personality so stubbornly and aggressively independent as Thoreau's would be a stumbling-block to many critics, good and bad alike, might have been foreseen, and indeed *was* foreseen, from the first. "What an easy task it would be," said one who understood him unusually well,[1] "for a lively and not entirely scrupulous pen to ridicule his notions, and raise such a cloud of ink in the clear medium as entirely to obscure his true and noble traits!" Just three months after these prophetic words were written appeared Lowell's well-known criticism of Thoreau in the *North American Review,* afterwards reprinted in *My Study Windows,* an essay which was a masterpiece of hostile innuendo and ingenious misrepresentation, written with all the cleverness and brilliancy of which its author was capable. Lowell, who had been one of Thoreau's fellow students at Harvard University, and had held friendly relations with him after the close of their college career, highly eulogised him in 1849, in the *Massachusetts Quarterly,* as one of those rare persons who, in a utilitarian age, can still feel and express the almost indefinable charm of wild nature, and further spoke of him in a tone of much personal friendliness. Ten years later, however, this friendly acquaintance was sharply terminated by a difference which arose, as already mentioned, about an article contributed by Thoreau to the *Atlantic Monthly,* then under Lowell's editorship; and we have had it stated, on Emerson's authority, that Lowell "never forgave Thoreau for having wounded his self-consciousness"—presumably in a correspondence that arose on this subject. I make no apology for calling attention to this nexus of events, because it furnishes the explanation of the otherwise strange animus which underlies Lowell's article. Brilliant as is the view obtained from *My Study Windows,* it ought to be more generally known that there is at least one pane therein which is discoloured and distorted, and which cannot be trusted by those literary students who would keep an unprejudiced outlook.[2]

"A skulker" is the phrase in which Mr. R. L. Stevenson summed up Thoreau's character in his essay in *Men and Books;* but as he himself admits in the later-written preface that he had quite misread Thoreau through lack of sufficient knowledge of his life, there is no reason why we should feel disturbed at the bestowal of that singularly inappropriate epithet; the marvel is that Stevenson should have deemed his blundering essay worth preservation. Other critics, again, while enjoying much of Thoreau's writing, have been haunted by a suspicion that he was the victim of a theatrical self-consciousness, and that he became a hermit rather to attract attention than to avoid it. "We have a mistrust of the sincerity of the St. Simeon Stylites," said a contemporary reviewer of *Walden,* "and suspect that they come down from their pillars in the night-time when nobody is looking at them. Diogenes placed his tub where Alexander would be sure of seeing it, and Mr. Thoreau ingenuously confesses that he went out to dine." So inconceivable does it seem to those who have not considered, much less practised, a simple and frugal life, that a man should deliberately, and for his own pleasure, abandon what *they* believe to be luxuries and comforts, that critics are always discovering some far-fetched and non-existent object in the Walden experiment, while they miss its true and salutary lessons.

Thoreau's "lack of ambition" is another point that has caused him to be much misunderstood—even Emerson gave his sanction to this rather futile complaint. "I cannot help counting it a fault in him," he said, "that he had no ambition. Wanting this, instead of engineering for all America, he was the captain of a huckleberry party. Pounding beans is good to the end of pounding empires one of these days; but if, at the end of years, it is still only beans!" But the obvious answer to this criticism is that, in Thoreau's case, it was *not* only beans. The chapter on "The Bean Field," in *Walden,* is one of the most imaginative and mystic in all his works—"it was no longer beans that I hoed," he says, "nor I that hoed beans"—for the object of his quest and labour was not the actual huckleberry nor the tangible bean, but the glorified and idealised fruit of a lifetime spent in communion with nature, which imparted to his writings a freshness and fragrance as of nature itself. In this matter Thoreau was the wiser judge of his own powers, and conferred a far greater benefit on the human race by writing *Walden* than he could have done by engineering for all America.

After all that has been said in this book of Thoreau's great debt to Emerson, it may, I think, be added without prejudice or ingratitude that the common misapprehension of Thoreau's character must be partly traced back to Emerson's "Biographical Sketch," and to his unfortunate manner of editing the Letters and Poems. That excessive insistence on Thoreau's "stoicism," to the subordination of his gentler and more affectionate traits, has done much to postpone a general recognition of the deep tenderness that underlay the rugged nature and rough sayings of the author of *Walden,* and we may be permitted to doubt whether Emerson had really gauged his friend's mind as fully as he imagined. That Thoreau, on his side, was sensible of Emerson's limitations, is proved by the opinion which he expressed to a friend that Emerson would be classed by posterity with Sir Thomas Browne—an estimate far lower than the usual one.

And here I would hazard the suggestion (though well aware that it must at present seem fantastic) that Thoreau's genius will eventually be even more highly valued than Emerson's. No sane critic could for a moment doubt the mighty influence which Emerson's great and beneficent intellect wielded among his contemporaries, or dream of comparing Thoreau with him as a nineteenth-century power. But the class of mind which has the most lasting hold on men's interest and homage is not always, and not often, the same as that which rules contemporary thought; and in the long run the race is to the most brilliant rather than to the most balanced of writers, to the poet rather than to the philosopher, to him who most keenly challenges the curiosity and imagination of his readers. Of all the Concord group, the most inspired, stimulating, and vital personality is Thoreau's; and when time has softened down the friction caused by superficial blemishes and misunderstandings, the world will realise that it was no mere Emersonian disciple, but a master-mind and heart of hearts who left that burning message to his fellow-men.

The sum of the whole matter is, that Thoreau had a clear and definite object before him which he followed with inflexible earnestness, and that his very faults and oddities subserved the main purpose of his life. "There is a providence in his writings," says John Weiss, "which ought to protect him from the complaint that he was not somebody else. No man ever lived who paid more ardent and unselfish attention to his business. If pure minds are sent into the world upon errands, with strict injunction not to stray by other paths, Thoreau certainly was one of these elect. A great deal of criticism is inspired by the inability to perceive the function and predestined quality of the man who passes in review. It only succeeds in explaining the difference between him and the critic. Such a decided fact as a man of genius is, ought to be gratefully accepted and interpreted."

That Thoreau's doctrines, no less than his character, have their shortcomings and imperfections, few will be disposed to deny. He could not realise, or perhaps did not care to realise, the immense scope and complexity of the whole social problem; he had scarcely the data or opportunities for doing so; and in any case his intensely individualistic nature would probably have incapacitated him. We therefore cannot look to him for any full and satisfactory solution of the difficulties by which our modern civilisation is surrounded, but it would be a great error to conclude that we are not to look to him at all. If it is true that the deadlock can never be relieved without external legislation, it is equally true that there can be no real regeneration of society without the self-improvement of the individual man; it is idle to assert that the one or the other must come first—*both* are necessary, and the two must be carried on side by side. In Thoreau the social instinct was deficient or undeveloped; but, on the other hand, he has set forth the gospel of the higher individualism with surpassing ability, and to him more than to any modern writer, can we apply Sir Henry Wotton's stanza:

> This man is freed from servile bands
> Of hope to rise, or fear to fall;
> Lord of himself, though not of lands,
> And having nothing, yet hath all.

We have seen that he was not, like Emerson, a philosopher of wide far-reaching sympathies and cautious judicial temperament, but rather a prophet and monitor—outspoken, unsparing, irreconcilable. He addressed himself to the correction of certain popular tendencies which he perceived to be mischievous and delusive, and preached what may be comprehensively termed a gospel of simplicity, in direct antagonism to the prevailing tone of a self-indulgent and artificial society. Who will venture to say that the protest was not needed then—that it is not still more needed now? "The years which have passed," Mr. Thomas Hughes has said, "since Thoreau came back out of Walden wood, to attend to his father's business of pencil-making, have added more than the previous century to the trappings and baggage of social life, which he held, and taught by precept and example, that men would be both better and happier for doing without. And while we succumb and fall year by year more under the dominion of these trappings, and life gets more and more overlaid with one kind and another of upholsteries, the idea of something simpler and nobler probably never haunted men's minds more than at this time." Herein lies the strength of Thoreau's position, that the very excess of the evil, which turns our supposed comforts into discomforts and our luxuries into burdens, must at last induce us to listen to the voice of sobriety and reason.

As to the manner in which Thoreau expresses his convictions nothing more need here be said, except that his style is justly adapted to his sentiments. His "knock-down blows at current opinion" are likened by Mr. R. L. Stevenson to the "posers" of a child, "which leave the orthodox in a kind of speechless agony." Thoreau is thus seen to have a quickening, stimulating, and, at times, exasperating effect as an ethical teacher; it is no part of his object to prophesy smooth things, to deal tenderly with the weaknesses of his readers, or even to explain those features of his doctrine which, from their novelty or unpopularity, are most likely to be misunderstood. This being so, his character and writings were certain to prove as distasteful to some readers as they are attractive to others; if he is a good deal misapplied at present, time will set that right.

In conclusion, we see in Thoreau the extraordinary product of an extraordinary era—his strange, self-centered, solitary figure, unique in the annals of literature, challenges attention by its originality, audacity, and independence. He had, it has been well remarked, "a constitutional *No* in him"; he renounced much that other men held dear, and set his heart on objects which to the world seemed valueless; it was part of his mission to question, to deny, to contradict. But his genius was not only of the negative and destructive order. In an age when not one man in a thousand had a real sympathy with nature, he attained to an almost miraculous acquaintance with her most cherished secrets; in an age of pessimism, when most men, as he himself expresses it, "lead lives of quiet desperation," he was filled with an absolute confidence in the justice and benevolence of his destiny; in an age of artificial complexity, when the ideal is unduly divorced from the practical, and society stands in false antagonism to nature, he, a devout pantheist, saw everywhere simplicity, oneness, relationship. In his view, God was not to be considered apart from the material world, nor was man to be set above and aloof from the rest of creation and the lower forms of life; he tracked everywhere the same divine intelligence—"inanimate" nature there was none, since all was instinct with the same universal spirit. It was his purpose, in a word, "to civilise nature with the highest intuitions of the mind, which show her simplicity to restless and artificial men."

This ideal he pursued, as we have seen, with a rare courage, sincerity, and self-devotion. His example and doctrines were coldly and incredulously received during his lifetime by most of those with whom he came in contact, and his comparatively early death cut him off, in the prime of his vigour, from reaping the harvest he had sown with such patience and assiduity; so far his career, like that of most idealists, must be confessed a failure. But these are not the tests by which idealists, least of all Thoreau, can be judged. For he enjoyed, in the first place, that priceless and inalienable success which consists in perfect serenity of mind and contentment with one's own fortunes. "If the day and night," he says in *Walden,* "are such that you greet them with joy, and life emits a fragrance like flowers and sweet-scented herbs—is more elastic, starry, and immortal—that is your success." And, secondly, he had the assurance, which is seldom denied to a great man, that the true value of his work would ultimately be recognised and appreciated. During the period that has passed since his death his fame has steadily increased both in America and England, and is destined to increase yet further.[3]

The blemishes and mannerisms of Thoreau's character are written on its surface, easy to be read by the indifferent passer-by who may miss the strong and sterling faculties that underlie them. His lack of geniality, his rusticity, his occasional sourness of tone and temper, his impatience of custom, degenerating sometimes into injustice, his too sensitive self-consciousness, his trick of over-statement in the expression of his views—these were incidental failings which did not mar the essential nobility of his nature. We shall do wisely in taking him just as he is, neither shutting our eyes to his defects nor greatly deploring their existence, but remembering that in so genuine and distinctive an individuality the "faults" have their due place and proportion no less than the "virtues." Had he added the merits he lacked to those which he possessed, had he combined the social with the individual qualities, had he been more catholic in his philosophy and more guarded in his expression, then we might indeed have admired him more, but should scarcely have loved him so well, for his character, whatever it gained in fulness, would have missed the peculiar freshness and piquancy which are now its chief attraction—whatever else he might have been, he would not have been Thoreau.

NOTES

1. John Weiss, *Christian Examiner,* July 1865.

2. "From the gentlemanly windows of the country seat no sincere eyes are directed upon nature." Thoreau's *Journal,* I, 255.

3. Witness the splendid "Walden" edition of his works, in twenty volumes, issued by his Boston publishers in 1906. Most noteworthy of all, perhaps, is the testimony of the many simple pilgrims who have been drawn to Concord by love of Thoreau's writings—the student named Harrington, for example, who came from Indiana in 1866, and told Channing that Thoreau's death had grieved him more, though a stranger, than that of any one he had known; or the Russian Jew who emigrated to America through having read some stray leaves of *Walden,* and whose greatest desire in life was to translate the book into his own tongue. It is the vital influence of this sort, far more than current "popularity," that makes its mark in the end.

APPENDIX

Portraits of Thoreau

There are three original portraits of Thoreau, which are familiar to readers in various forms.

1. Henry David Thoreau in 1854. Crayon sketch by Rowse. The photographic copy of the sketch was made by A. W. (Fred) Hosmer and is now in the Rare Book and Special Collections Library, University of Illinois at Urbana-Champaign.

2. Henry David Thoreau in 1856. Daguerreotype by B. D. Maxham. The photographic copy of the daguerreotype was made by A. W. (Fred) Hosmer and is now in the Rare Book and Special Collections Library, University of Illinois at Urbana-Champaign.

3. Henry David Thoreau in 1861. Ambrotype by E. S. Dunshee. The photographic copy of the ambrotype was made by A. W. (Fred) Hosmer and is now in the Rare Book and Special Collections Library, University of Illinois at Urbana-Champaign.

Bibliography by John P. Anderson (British Museum), 1896 with Salt's added entries, 1908

Works

A Week on the Concord and Merrimack Rivers. Boston, 1849, 12mo.

——— Another edition. Boston, 1862, 12mo.

——— New and revised edition. Boston, 1867, 16mo.

——— Another edition. With a Prefatory Note by Will H. Dircks. London [1889], 12mo.

——— Riverside edition. Vol. i. Boston and New York, 1894, 12mo.

Walden; or, Life in the Woods. Boston, 1854, 12mo. Re-issued in 1864.

——— Another edition. Edinburgh, 1884, 8vo.

——— Another edition. With an Introductory Note by Will H. Dircks. London, 1886, 12mo. Part of the "Camelot Series."

——— Another edition. 2 vols. Boston, 1889, 12mo. Part of the "Riverside Aldine Series."

——— Riverside edition, vol. ii. Boston and New York, 1894, 8vo.

——— Another edition. With an Introductory Note by Will H. Dircks. London [1895], 8vo.

Excursions. Boston, 1863, 12mo. [Edited by R. W. Emerson and Sophia Thoreau, with a biographical sketch by the former.]

——— Riverside edition, vol. ix. Boston and New York, 1894, 8vo.

The Maine Woods. Boston, 1864, 12mo.

——— Riverside edition, vol. iii. Boston and New York, 1894, 8vo.

Cape Cod. [Edited by Sophia Thoreau and William Ellery Channing.] Boston, 1865, 12mo.

——— Another edition. London, 1865, 12mo.

——— Another edition. Boston, 1892, 8vo.

——— Riverside edition, vol. iv. Boston and New York, 1894, 8vo.

Letters to Various Persons. [Edited by R. W. Emerson.] Boston, 1865, 12mo.

A Yankee in Canada, with Anti-Slavery and Reform Papers. [Edited by Sophia Thoreau and William Ellery Channing.] Boston, 1866, 12mo.

Early Spring in Massachusetts. From the Journal of Henry D. Thoreau. [Edited by H. G. O. Blake.] Boston, 1881, 12mo.

——— Riverside edition, vol. v. Boston and New York, 1894, 8 vo.

Summer: From the Journal of Henry D. Thoreau. Edited by H. G. O. Blake. Boston, 1884, 12mo.

——— Another edition. London, 1884, 8vo.

——— Riverside edition, vol. vi. Boston and New York, 1894, 8vo.

Winter: From the Journal of Henry D. Thoreau. Edited by H. G. O. Blake. Boston, 1888, 12mo.

——— Riverside edition, vol. viii. Edited by H. G. O. Blake. Boston and New York, 1894, 8vo.

Autumn: From the Journal of Henry D. Thoreau. Edited by H. G. O. Blake. Boston, 1892, 12mo.

——— Riverside edition, vol. vii. Edited by H. G. O. Blake. Boston and New York, 1894, 8vo.

Miscellanies. With a biographical sketch, by Ralph Waldo Emerson, and a general index to the writings. Boston and New York, 1894, 8vo. Vol. x. of the Riverside edition.

Familiar Letters of Henry David Thoreau. Edited, with an Introduction and Notes, by F. B. Sanborn. Boston and New York, 1894, 8vo. Vol. xi. of the Riverside edition.

Selections

The Succession of Forest Trees, Wild Apples, and Sounds. With a biographical sketch by Ralph Waldo Emerson. Boston, 1887, 8vo. No. 27 of the "Riverside Literature Series." The first two papers and Emerson's sketch are from *Excursions;* the third paper is from *Walden.*

Anti-Slavery and Reform Papers by Henry D. Thoreau. Selected and edited by H. S. Salt. London, 1890, 8vo.

Essays and other Writings of Henry Thoreau. Edited, with a Prefatory Note, by Will H. Dircks. London [1891], 8vo. Part of the "Camelot Series."

Thoreau's Thoughts. Selections from the Writings of Henry David Thoreau. Edited by H. G. O. Blake. [With a bibliography.] Boston and New York, 1894, 12mo.

Selections from Thoreau. Edited, with an introduction, by H. S. Salt. London, 1895, 8vo.

Poems of Nature. Edited by H. S. Salt and F. B. Sanborn. London, Boston and New York, 1895, 8vo.

Contributions to Magazines, Etc.

Dial, vol. i., 1840.—Sympathy, "Lately alas! I knew a gentle boy," pp. 71, 72; reprinted in *A Week on the Concord and Merrimack Rivers.*

——— Aulus Persius Flaccus, pp. 117–121; reprinted in *A Week on the Concord and Merrimack Rivers.*

——— Stanzas, "Nature doth have her dawn each day;" reprinted in *A Week on the Concord and Merrimack Rivers.*

——— Vol. ii., 1841.—Sic Vita, "I am a parcel of vain strivings tied," p. 81; reprinted in *A Week on the Concord and Merrimack Rivers.*

——— Friendship, "Let such pure hate still under-prop," pp. 204, 205; reprinted in *A Week on the Concord and Merrimack Rivers.*

——— Vol. iii., 1842.—Natural History of Massachusetts, pp. 19–40; reprinted in *Excursions.*

——— Stanzas, "Great God, I ask Thee for no meaner pelf," pp. 79, 80; reprinted in *A Yankee in Canada.*

——— The Black Knight, "Be sure your fate," p. 180; reprinted in Riverside edition, vol. x.

——— The Inward Morning, "Packed in my mind lie all the clothes," p. 198; reprinted in *A Week on the Concord and Merrimack Rivers.*

——— Free Love, "My love must be as free," p. 199; reprinted in *A Week on the Concord and Merrimack Rivers.*

——— The Poet's Delay, "In vain I see the morning rise," p. 200; reprinted in *A Week on the Concord and Merrimack Rivers.*

——— Rumours from an Æolian Harp, p. 200; reprinted in *A Week on the Concord and Merrimack Rivers.*

——— The Moon, "The full-orbed moon with unchanging ray," p. 222; reprinted in Riverside edition, vol. x.

——— To the Maiden in the East, "Low in the Eastern sky," pp. 222–224; reprinted in *A Week on the Concord and Merrimack Rivers.*

——— The Summer Rain, "My books I'd fain cast off, I cannot read," pp. 224, 225; reprinted in *A Week on the Concord and Merrimack Rivers.*

——— The Laws of Menu, selected by Thoreau, pp. 331–340.

——— The Prometheus Bound, a translation, pp. 363–386; reprinted in Riverside edition, vol. x.

——— Anacreon, eleven poems translated, pp. 484–490; reprinted in *A Week on the Concord and Merrimack Rivers.*

——— Sayings of Confucius, selected, pp. 493, 494.

——— To a Stray Fowl, "Poor bird! destined to lead thy life," p. 505; reprinted in Riverside edition, vol. x.

——— Orphics, i. Smoke; ii. Haze, pp. 505, 506; reprinted in *Letters to Various Persons.*

——— Dark Ages, pp. 527–529; reprinted in *A Week on the Concord and Merrimack Rivers.*

——— Friendship. From Chaucer's "Romaunt of the Rose," pp. 529–531.

——— Vol. iv., 1843.—Ethnical Scriptures. Chinese four books, selected by Thoreau, pp. 205–210.

——— A Winter Walk, pp. 211–226; reprinted in *Excursions.*

——— Homer, Ossian, Chaucer, pp. 290–303, reprinted in *A Week on the Concord and Merrimack Rivers.*

——— Pindar, note and translations, pp. 379–390; reprinted in Riverside edition, vol. x.

——— The Preaching of Buddha, selections, pp. 391–404.

——— Ethnical Scriptures. Hermes Trismegistus, selections, pp. 402–404.

——— Herald of Freedom, pp. 507–512; reprinted in *A Yankee in Canada.*

——— Fragments of Pindar, pp. 513, 514; reprinted in Riverside edition, vol. x.

The Boston Miscellany, 1843.—A Walk to Wachusett, vol. iii., p. 51; reprinted in *Excursions.*

The Democratic Review, 1843.—The Landlord, vol. xiii., pp. 427–430; reprinted in *Excursions.*

——— Paradise (to be) Regained, vol. xiii., pp. 451–463; reprinted in *A Yankee in Canada.*

The Liberator. —Wendell Phillips before the Concord Lyceum, March 28, 1845; reprinted in *A Yankee in Canada.*

——— Slavery in Massachusetts, an address delivered (July 4) at the Anti-Slavery Celebration at Framingham, July 21, 1854; reprinted in *A Yankee in Canada.*

——— The Last Days of John Brown. Read (July 4) at North Elba, N. Y., July 27, 1860.

Graham's Magazine, 1845.—Thomas Carlyle and his Works, vol. xxx., pp. 145, 238; reprinted in *A Yankee in Canada.*

The Union Magazine, 1845.—Ktaadn and the Maine Woods, vol. iii., pp. 29, 73, 132, 177, 216; reprinted in *The Maine Woods.*

Æsthetic Papers, 1849.—Resistance to Civil Government, pp. 189–211; reprinted in *A Yankee in Canada.*

Putnam's Magazine, 1853–55.—An Excursion to Canada, vol. i., pp. 54–59, 179–184, 321–329; reprinted in *A Yankee in Canada.*

——— Cape Cod, vol. v., pp. 632–640; vol. vi., pp. 59–66, 157–164; reprinted in *Cape Cod.*

The New York Tribune, 1860.—The Succession of Forest Trees (read before the Middlesex Agricultural Society, Concord, Sept. 1860); reprinted in *Excursions.*

Echoes of Harper's Ferry, by James Redpath, 1860.—A Plea for Captain John Brown, read to the citizens of Concord, Mass., Oct. 30, 1859, pp. 16–42; reprinted in *A Yankee in Canada.*

——— Remarks at Concord on the day of the Execution of John Brown (Dec. 2, 1860), pp. 439–445; reprinted in Riverside edition, vol. x.

Atlantic Monthly, 1858–93.—Chesuncook, vol. ii., 1858, pp. 2–12, 224–233, 305–317; reprinted in *The Maine Woods.*

——— Walking, vol. ix., 1862, pp. 657–674; reprinted in *Excursions.*

——— Autumnal Tints, vol. x., 1862, pp. 385–402; reprinted in *Excursions.*

——— Wild Apples, vol. x., 1862, pp. 513–526; reprinted in *Excursions.*

——— Life without Principle, vol. xii., 1863, pp. 484–495; reprinted in *A Yankee in Canada.*

——— Night and Morning, vol. xii., 1863, pp. 579–583; reprinted in *Excursions.*

——— The Wellfleet Oysterman, vol. xiv., 1864, pp. 470–478; reprinted in *Cape Cod.*

——— The Highland Light, vol. xiv., 1864, pp. 649–659; reprinted in *Cape Cod.*

——— April Days, vol. xli., 1878, pp. 445–454; reprinted in Riverside edition, vol. v.

——— May Days, vol. xli., 1878, pp. 567–576; reprinted in Riverside edition, vol. ix.

——— Days in June, vol. xli., 1878, pp. 711–719; reprinted in Riverside edition, vol. v.

——— Winter Days, vol. lv., 1885, pp. 79–88; reprinted in Riverside edition, vol. viii.

The Boston Commonwealth, 1863. Poems.—Inspiration, vol. i., No. 42; The Funeral Bell, vol. i., No. 44; Travelling: Greece, vol. i., No. 47; The Departure, vol. i., No. 52; The Fall of the Leaf, vol. ii., No. 58; Independence, vol. ii., No. 61; The Soul's Season, vol. ii., No. 62.

Appendix
Biography, Criticism, Etc.

Alcott, A. Bronson.—Concord Days. Boston, 1872, 8vo. Thoreau, pp. 11–20; Walden Pond, pp. 259–263.

——— Sonnets and Canzonets. Boston, 1882, 8vo. Thoreau, Sonnet xiv., p. 121.

Alger, William R.—The Solitudes of Nature and of Man. Boston, 1867, 8vo. Thoreau, pp. 329–338.

Allibone, S. Austin.—A critical dictionary of English Literature, etc. London, 1871, 8vo. Thoreau, vol. iii., pp. 2406, 2407.

Barton, W. G.—Thoreau, Flagg, and Burroughs. (*Essex Institute, Historical Collections,* vol. xxii., pp. 53–80.) Salem, Mass., 1885, 8vo.

Beers, Henry A.—An outline sketch of American Literature. New York, 1887, 12mo. Numerous references to Thoreau.

Besant, Walter.—The Eulogy of Richard Jefferies. London, 1888, 8vo. Reference to Thoreau, pp. 221–225.

Brown, John.—The Life and Letters of John Brown. Edited by F. B. Sanborn. London, 1885, 8vo. Numerous references to Thoreau.

Burroughs, John.—Indoor Studies. Boston, 1889, 8vo. Henry D. Thoreau, pp. 1–42.

Channing, William Ellery.—Thoreau: the poet-naturalist. Boston, 1873, 8vo.

Conway, Moncure Daniel.—Emerson at Home and Abroad. Boston, 1882, 8vo. Thoreau, pp. 279–289.

Cooke, George Willis.—Ralph Waldo Emerson: his life, writings, and philosophy. London, 1882, 8vo. Numerous references to Thoreau.

Critic.—Essays from "The Critic." Boston, 1882, 12mo. Thoreau's Wildness, by John Burroughs, pp. 9–18; Thoreau's unpublished poetry, by F. B. Sanborn, pp. 71–78.

Curtis, George William.—Homes of American Authors. New York, 1857, 8vo. Thoreau, pp. 247, 248, 250, 251.

——— From the Easy Chair. London, 1892, 12mo. Thoreau and my Lady Cavaliere, pp. 62–73.

Duyckinck, Evert A., and George L.—Cyclopædia of American Literature, 2 vols. Philadelphia, 1877, 8vo. Henry David Thoreau, vol. ii., pp. 601–604.

Ellis, Havelock.—The New Spirit. London, 1890, 8vo. Thoreau, pp. 90–99.

Emerson, Edward Waldo.—Emerson in Concord: a Memoir written for the "Social Circle" in Concord, Massachusetts. London, 1889, 8vo. Numerous references to Thoreau.

Emerson, Ralph Waldo.—Lectures and Biographical Sketches. London, 1884, 8vo. Thoreau, pp. 419–452; prefixed also to Thoreau's *Excursions.*

——— The Complete Works of Ralph Waldo Emerson (Centenary Edition). Boston, 1904. 12 vols.

Encyclopædia Britannica.—Encyclopædia Britannica, 9th edition. Edinburgh, 1888, 4to. Henry D. Thoreau, by William Sharp, vol. 23, pp. 313, 314.

Essays.—Essays from "The Critic." Boston, 1882, 8vo. Thoreau's Wildness. By John Burroughs, pp. 9–18. Thoreau's unpublished poetry. By F. B. Sanborn, pp. 71–78.

Flagg, Wilson.—The Woods and By-ways of New England. Boston, 1872, 8vo. Thoreau, pp. 392–396.

——— Halcyon Days. Boston, 1881, 8vo. Thoreau, pp. 164–168.

Garnett, Richard.—Life of Ralph Waldo Emerson. London, 1888, 8vo. Thoreau, pp. 157–159.

Graham, P. Anderson.—Nature in Books; some Studies in Biography. London, 1891, 8vo. The Philosophy of Idleness (Henry David Thoreau), pp. 66–93.

Griswold, R. W.—Prose Writers of America. Philadelphia [1870], 8vo. Thoreau, p. 657.

Haskins, David Greene.—Ralph Waldo Emerson; his maternal ancestors, etc. London [1887], 8vo. Henry D. Thoreau, pp. 119–122.

Hawthorne, Julian.—Nathaniel Hawthorne and his wife: a biography. 2 vols. London, 1885, 8vo. References to Thoreau.

Hawthorne, Nathaniel.—Passages from the American Note-Books. 2 vols. Boston, 1868, 8vo. References to Thoreau, vol ii., pp. 96–99, 110–113, 123.

Higginson, Thomas Wentworth.—Short Studies of American Authors. Boston, 1888, 8vo. Thoreau, pp. 22–31.

Holmes, Oliver Wendell.—American Men of Letters. Ralph Waldo Emerson. Boston, 1885, 8vo. Numerous references to Thoreau.

Hubert, Philip G.—Liberty and a Living. New York, 1889, 8vo. Thoreau, pp. 171–190.

James, Henry.—Hawthorne. (*English Men of Letters.*) London, 1879, 8vo. Thoreau, pp. 96–99.

Jones, Samuel Arthur.—Thoreau: a Glimpse. Ann Arbor, Mich., 1890, 8vo. Privately printed.

——— Bibliography of Henry David Thoreau, with an outline of his life. Compiled and chronologically arranged by S. A. Jones. New York, 1894, 8vo.

Lowell, James Russell. A Fable for Critics. [New York] 1848, 8vo. Thoreau, p. 32.

——— My Study Windows. Second edition. London, 1871, 8vo. Thoreau, pp. 145–156.

Nichol, John.—American Literature: an historical sketch. Edinburgh, 1882, 8vo. Henry D. Thoreau, pp. 313–321.

Page, H. A., *i.e.* A. H. Japp.—Thoreau, his Life and Aims. London, 1878, 8vo.

Richardson, Charles F.—American Literature, 1607–1885. 2 vols. New York, 1887–89, 8vo. References to Thoreau.

Salt, H. S.—Literary Sketches. London, 1888, 8vo. Henry D. Thoreau, pp. 124–166. Appeared originally in Temple Bar, Nov. 1886.

Sanborn, F. B.—American Men of Letters. Henry D. Thoreau. Boston, 1882, 8vo.

——— The Genius and character of Emerson; lectures at the Concord School of Philosophy. Boston, 1885, 8vo. References to Thoreau.

Scudder, Horace E.—American Prose. Boston, 1880, 8vo. Henry David Thoreau, pp. 296–301.

Stedman, Edmund Clarence.—A Library of American Literature. New York, 1891, 8vo. Thoreau, vol. xi., p. 594.

Stevenson, Robert Louis.—Familiar Studies of Men and Books. London, 1882, 8vo. Henry David Thoreau; his character and opinions, pp. 129–171; a reprint of article in *Cornhill,* June 1880.

Stewart, George.—Thoreau; the Hermit of Walden. A paper read before the Society, March 2nd, 1882. (*Trans. of the Literary and Hist. Soc. of Quebec,* No. 16, 1882, pp. 121–151.) Quebec, 1882, 8vo.

Triggs, Oscar L.—Browning and Whitman. London, 1893, 8vo. Thoreau, pp. 35–37.

Underwood, Francis H.—The Builders of American Literature. First Series. London, 1893, 8vo. Henry David Thoreau, pp. 213–216.

Welsh, Alfred H.—Development of English Literature and Language. 2 vols. Chicago, 1882, 8vo. Thoreau, vol. ii. pp. 402–414.

Woodbury, Charles J.—Talks with Ralph Waldo Emerson, London, 1890, 8vo. Thoreau, pp. 76–95.

Wilson, James Grant and Fiske, John.—Appleton's Cyclopædia of American Biography. 6 vols. New York, 1887–89, 8vo. Thoreau, vol. vi. pp. 100, 101.

Wolfe, Theodore F.—Literary Shrines; the haunts of some famous American authors. Philadelphia, 1895, 8vo. Numerous references to Thoreau.

Magazine Articles, Etc.

Thoreau, Henry David.—Atlantic Monthly, by R. W. Emerson, vol. 10, 1862, pp. 239–249.—Boston Commonwealth, vol. 1, No. 33, 1863.—Monthly Religious Magazine, by W. R. Alger, vol. 35, 1865, p. 382.—Christian Examiner, by J. Weiss, vol. 79, 1865, pp. 96–117.—Fraser's Magazine, by Moncure D. Conway, vol. 73, 1866, pp. 447–465; same article, Eclectic Magazine, vol. 4 N. S., 1866, pp. 180–195.—Every Saturday, by J. R. Lowell, vol. 10, 1870, p. 166.—British Quarterly Review, by Dr. A. H. Japp, vol. 59, 1874, pp. 181–194; same article, Littell's Living Age, vol. 120, pp. 643–650, and Eclectic Magazine, vol. 19 N. S., pp. 305–312.—Harper's New Monthly Magazine, by Miss H. R. Hudson, vol. 51, 1875, pp. 28–31.—Dublin University Magazine, by M. Collins, vol. 90, 1877, pp. 610–621.—Harvard Register (with portrait), by F. B. Sanborn, vol. 3, 1881, pp. 214–217.—Century (with portrait), by J. Burroughs, vol. 2 N. S., 1882, pp. 368–379.—Dial (Chicago), by H. N.

Powers, vol. 3, 1882, pp. 70, 71.—Spectator, vol. 56, 1883, pp. 239, 240; vol. 56, 1885, pp. 122, 123.—Temple Bar, by H. S. Salt, vol. 78, 1886, pp. 369–383; same article in Critic, vol. 8 N. S., pp. 276–278, 289–291; and Eclectic Magazine, vol. 45 N. S., pp. 89–98.—Welcome, by A. H. Japp, vol. 14, 1887, pp. 652–656.—Academy, by W. Lewin, October 25, 1890, pp. 357, 358.—Chautauquan, by John Burroughs, vol. 9, 1889, pp. 530–533.—Good Words, by F. H. Underwood, vol. 29, 1888, pp. 445–452.—Belgravia, vol. 81, 1893, pp. 375–383.—Labour Prophet (with portrait), by John Trevor, vol. 2, 1893, p. 190.—Lippincott's Magazine, by C. C. Abbott, June 1895, pp. 852–855.—Great Thoughts, by W. J. Jupp, January 19 and 26, 1895, pp. 256–258, 268, 287.

——— *An American Diogenes.* Chamber's Journal, vol. 8, 1858, pp. 330–332.

——— *An American Rousseau.* Saturday Review, vol. 18, 1864, pp. 694, 695.

——— *and his Biographers.* Lippincott's Magazine, by S. A. Jones, vol. 48, 1891, pp. 224–228.

——— *and his Books.* Harvard Magazine, by Edwin Morton, vol. 1, 1855, p. 87, etc.

——— *and his Works.* Inlander, by S. A. Jones, vol. 4, 1894, p. 234.

——— *and New England Transcendentalism.* Catholic World, by J. V. O'Conor, vol. 27, 1878, pp. 289–300.

——— *and Thomas Cholmondeley.* Atlantic Monthly, by F. B. Sanborn, vol. 72, 1893, pp. 741–756.

——— *Anti-Slavery and Reform Papers.* Lippincott's Magazine, by H. S. Salt, vol. 46, 1890, pp. 277–283.

——— *a Rural Humbug.* Knickerbocker, vol. 45, 1855, pp. 235–241.

——— *Autumn.* Vassar Miscellany, vol. 22, 1892, p. 92.

——— *Cape Cod.* Boston Commonwealth, vol. 3, No. 30, 1865.

——— *Channing's Life of.* Nation, vol. 18, 1874, pp. 29, 30.

——— *Character and Opinions of.* Cornhill Magazine, by R. L. Stevenson, vol. 41, 1880, pp. 665–682; same article, Eclectic Magazine, vol. 95, pp. 257–270, and Littell's Living Age, vol. 146, pp. 179–190.

——— *Correspondence with Emerson.* Atlantic Monthly, by F. B. Sanborn, vol. 69, 1892, pp. 577–596, 736–753.

——— *Days and Nights in Concord.* Scribner's Monthly, by W. E. Channing, vol. 16, 1878, pp. 721–728.

——— *Excursions.* Boston Commonwealth, vol. 2, No. 60, 1863.

——— *A Faithful Lover of Nature.* Frank R. Leslie's Popular Monthly, by W. Lincoln J. Adams, vol. 33, 1892, p. 574.

——— *Flute* (Poem). Atlantic Monthly, by Louisa M. Alcott, vol. 12, 1863, pp. 280, 281.

——— *The Forester.* Atlantic Monthly, by A. B. Alcott, vol. 9, pp. 443–445.

——— *A Glimpse.* Unitarian, by S. A. Jones, vol. 5, February-April.

——— *Gospel of Simplicity.* Paternoster Review, by H. S. Salt, vol. 1, 1891, pp. 461–468.

——— *Inheritance of.* Inlander, by S. A. Jones, vol. 3, 1892, p. 199.

——— *Letters to Various Persons.* Atlantic Monthly, by T. W. Higginson, vol. 16, 1865, pp. 504, 505.—North American Review, by J. R. Lowell, vol. 101, 1865, pp. 597–608.

——— *Life of,* by H. S. Salt. Spectator, by A. H. Japp, Oct. 18, 1890, pp. 526, 527.—Animal World, Dec. 1890, pp. 186, 187.

——— *The Maine Woods.* Boston Commonwealth, vol. 3, No. 30, 1864.—Atlantic Monthly, by T. W. Higginson, vol. 14, 1864, pp. 386, 387.

——— *Nature Notes.* Selborne Society's Journal, by J. L. Otter, vol. 1, 1890, p. 185.

——— *New Estimate of.* Penn Monthly, by W. S. Kennedy, vol. 11, pp. 794, etc.

——— *Page's Life of.* Academy, by Thomas Hughes, Nov. 17, 1877, pp. 462, 463.

——— *Philosophy at Concord.* Nation, Sept. 2, 1880, pp. 164–166.

——— *Pity and Humour of* (from the Spectator). Littell's Living Age, vol. 146, 1880, pp. 190, 191.

——— *Poems of Nature.* Scribner's Magazine, by F. B. Sanborn, March 1895, pp. 352–355.—Saturday Review, Jan. 18, 1896; Star, Jan. 23, 1896, by Richard Le Gallienne.

——— *Poetry of.* Lippincott's Magazine, by J. Benton, vol. 37, 1886, pp. 491–500.—Art Review, by H. S. Salt, May 1890, pp. 153–155.

——— *Portrait of, by Himself.* Literary World (Boston), March 26, 1881.

——— *Portraits of, with a Beard.* Critic, vol. 1, 1881, p. 95.

——— *Sanborn's Life of.* Nation, by A. G. Sedgwick, vol. 35, 1882, pp. 34, 35.—Literary World (Boston), vol. 13, 1882, pp. 227, 228.—Athenæum, Oct. 28, 1882, pp. 558–560.—Academy, by J. Purves, Oct. 14, 1882, pp. 271, 272.—American, by T. A. Janvier, vol. 4, 1882, p. 218.

——— *Selections from, H. S. Salt's.* Academy, by Walter Lewin, May 4, 1895, p. 377.

——— *Some Recollections and Incidents concerning.* Concord Freeman, by Joseph Hosmer, October 1880.

——— *Study of.* Eclectic Magazine (from the Academy), by Thomas Hughes, vol. 27 N. S., 1878, pp. 114–116.

——— *Summer.* Academy, by Walter Lewin, Sept. 27, 1884, pp. 193, 194.—Literary World (Boston), July 12, 1884, p. 223.—The Nation, vol. 39, 1884, pp. 98–99.

——— *Sunday at Concord.* Fortnightly Review, by Grant Allen, vol. 43, N. S., 1888, pp. 675–690.

——— *Ten Volumes of.* New Englander, by Joshua W. Caldwell, vol. 55, 1891, pp. 404–424.
Unpublished Poetry of (with portrait). Critic, by F. B. Sanborn, March 26, 1881, pp. 75, 76.
Visit to Walden Pond. Natural Food, by Hector Waylen, July 1895, pp. 438, 439.
——— *Walden.* Putnam's Monthly, by C. F. Briggs, vol. 4, 1854, pp. 443–448.—Boston Commonwealth, vol. 1, No. 56, 1863.
——— *Walden Pond.* Boston Commonwealth, vol. 3, No. 47, 1865.
——— *Week on the Concord.* Massachusetts Quarterly Review, by J. R. Lowell, vol. 3, 1849, pp. 40–51.—Saturday Review, August 17, 1889, pp. 195, 196.
——— *Wildness of.* Critic, by J. Burroughs, March 26, 1881, p. 74.
——— *Works of.* New Englander, by J. W. Caldwell, vol. 55, 1891, pp. 404–424.

Chronological List of Works

A Week on the Concord and Merrimack Rivers	1849
Walden; or, Life in the Woods	1854
Excursions	1863
The Maine Woods	1864
Cape Cod	1864
Letters to Various Persons	1865
A Yankee in Canada	1866
Early Spring in Massachusetts: From the Journal of Henry D. Thoreau	1881
Summer: From the Journal of Henry D. Thoreau	1884
Winter: From the Journal of Henry D. Thoreau	1888
Autumn: From the Journal of Henry D. Thoreau	1892
Miscellanies	1894
Familiar Letters	1894
Poems of Nature	1895
The Writings of Henry David Thoreau	1906

Added Entries, 1908

Allen, Francis H.—A Bibliography of Henry David Thoreau. Boston, 1908.
Anon.—*Reminiscences of Thoreau.* Outlook, December 2, 1899.
Channing, William Ellery.—Thoreau, the Poet-Naturalist, ed. by F. B. Sanborn. Boston, 1902.

Emerson, Ralph Waldo. *The Complete Works* (Centenary Edition). Boston, 1904. 12 vols.

Gilchrist, H. H.—Anne Gilchrist: Her Life and Writings. London, 1887.

Jones, Samuel Arthur.—*An Afternoon in the University Library.* Inlander 1, pp. 150–153.

——— Some Unpublished Letters of Henry D. and Sophia E. Thoreau, Jamaica, N. Y., 1899.

——— *Thoreau's Incarceration.* Inlander vol. 9, December 1898, pp. 96–103.

——— *Vox Clamantis in Deserto.* Inlander, March 1898, pp. 222–230.

Ricketson, Anna and Walton, editors—Daniel Ricketson and His Friends. Boston, 1902.

Salt, H. S.—The Life of Henry David Thoreau. London, 1890, 8vo. Second edition, 1896.

Sanborn, F. B.—Personality of Thoreau. Boston, 1901.

Traubel, Horace.—With Walt Whitman in Camden. Boston, 1906.

Whitman, Walt—Specimen Days. Philadelphia, 1882.

Williams, Henry—Memorials of the Class of 1837. Boston, 1887.

Wright, M. B.—*Uncle Peter.* Boston Transcript, February 8, 1896.

The Writings of Henry David Thoreau (Walden Edition). Boston, 1906. 20 vols.

Index

UNIVERSITY OF ILLINOIS PRESS
1325 SOUTH OAK STREET
CHAMPAIGN, ILLINOIS 61820-6903
WWW.PRESS.UILLINOIS.EDU